Busy Mum's
BAKING
Book

WENDY CRAIG

Busy Mum's BAKING Book

HAMLYN

Jacket photograph by Jeany Savage
Inside photography by Dave Jordon
Decorative illustrations by Robin Lawrie
Diagrams by Joyce Tuhill

Published in 1985 by
Hamlyn Publishing
Bridge House, London Road
Twickenham, Middlesex, England

© Hamlyn Publishing 1985
a division of The Hamlyn Publishing Group Ltd

ISBN 0 600 32479 6

Set in 10/12 pt Palatino
by Wyvern Typesetting Limited, Bristol

Printed in Italy

Contents

Useful Facts and Figures

Notes on metrication

In this book quantities are given in metric and Imperial measures. Exact conversion from Imperial to metric measures does not usually give very convenient working quantities and so the metric measures have been rounded off into units of 25 grams. The table below shows the recommended equivalents.

Ounces	Approx g to nearest whole figure	Recommended conversion to nearest unit of 25	Ounces	Approx g to nearest whole figure	Recommended conversion to nearest unit of 25
1	28	25	9	255	250
2	57	50	10	283	275
3	85	75	11	312	300
4	113	100	12	340	350
5	142	150	13	368	375
6	170	175	14	396	400
7	198	200	15	425	425
8	227	225	16 (1 lb)	454	450

Note: When converting quantities over 20 oz first add the appropriate figures in the centre column, then adjust to the nearest unit of 25. As a general guide, 1 kg (1000 g) equals 2·2 lb or about 2 lb 3 oz. This method of conversion gives good results in nearly all cases, although in certain pastry and cake recipes a more accurate conversion is necessary to produce a balanced recipe.

Liquid measures. The millilitre has been used in this book and the following table gives a few examples.

Imperial	Approx ml to nearest whole figure	Recommended ml	Imperial	Approx ml to nearest whole figure	Recommended ml
¼ pint	142	150 ml	1 pint	567	600 ml
½ pint	283	300 ml	1½ pints	851	900 ml
¾ pint	425	450 ml	1¾ pints	992	1000 ml (1 litre)

Spoon measures. All spoon measures given in this book are level unless otherwise stated.

Can sizes. At present, cans are marked with the exact (usually to the nearest whole number) metric equivalent of the Imperial weight of the contents, so we have followed this practice when giving can sizes.

Oven temperatures

The table below gives recommended equivalents.

	°C	°F	Gas Mark		°C	°F	Gas Mark
Very cool	110	225	¼	Moderately	190	375	5
	120	250	½	hot	200	400	6
Cool	140	275	1	Hot	220	425	7
	150	300	2		230	450	8
Moderate	160	325	3	Very hot	240	475	9
	180	350	4				

Note: When making any of the recipes in this book, only follow one set of measures as they are not interchangeable.

Introduction

One of my happiest childhood memories is that of coming home from school to find the house suffused with the delightful aroma of baking. My mother had probably spent the afternoon sieving flour, beating eggs and concocting some delicious tea-time delights for her hungry family. The kitchen would be warm from the oven and there on the table would stand a proud array of biscuits, pies, scones and cakes. Nothing has ever matched the cosy, contented feeling that the smell of baking gives me.

It was at my mother's elbow that I first learned the rudiments of baking. She gave me the scraps of pastry which I kneaded until they were pale grey and grubby. I learned to roll them out, cut them into shapes and bake them. My poor father had to pretend that these grimy rock hard offerings were delicious, just as many fathers do. Later in domestic science classes I was taught how to make scones and rock cakes in an extremely sterile and efficient atmosphere, but somehow they were never quite as good as the things I made in Mum's kitchen. She knew we had favourites and she baked them when she felt we deserved a reward. My brother's favourite was a three-layer chocolate cake with vanilla butter cream spread thickly between the layers and soft chocolate icing rippling over the crown; mine was apple-pie. Oh, that scrumptious shortcrust and the mouth-watering scent of Bramleys with just a hint of cloves.

One of the most comforting things about baking is the sense of continuity and order it brings. The yearly cycle and all its traditions are encapsulated within the floury fingers of the home baker. The wonderful fruit pies of autumn are replaced by mince pies and Christmas cake, which in turn make way for spring pasties, simnel cake and hot cross buns, and they in turn are followed by summer quiches and strawberry flans. Of course, nowadays, we can have any of these things at anytime, but I'll wager you won't feel like eating crumpets on a hot summer's day.

Intended for busy mothers with hungry families, these recipes are quick, inexpensive and they might give you ideas of your own to fill those ever open beaks. Encourage your youngsters to help; it will be a happy experience for them to share a warm kitchen with you and, of course, do let them clean out the dish and lick the spoon. Memories are made of this.

Pies, Flans and Pastries

Steaming hot savoury pies make perfect, warming winter meals for hungry families. They are also good for preparing in advance, ready to pop in the oven just in time for dinner. Traditional favourites, like Steak and Kidney Pie and a Cheesy Fish Pie, are included here along with lots of ideas to make plain pastry more interesting.

There are flans and pasties too, both savoury and sweet; many of these taste just as good cold as they do when they are hot from the oven. So if you want to make a quick savoury flan in the morning and set it aside to have with salad for supper, then you'll find some ideas in this chapter. There is also a recipe for picnic pie which is a sure winner when it comes to eating out of doors.

Shortcrust Pastry

225 g/8 oz plain flour · pinch of salt
100 g/4 oz margarine · 2 tablespoons cold water

Shortcrust pastry should be crisp and short with a fine even texture. The pastry should be handled quickly and lightly, and chilling it before cooking helps to give a good short texture.

Place the flour and salt in a bowl. Add the margarine and rub in lightly with the fingertips until the mixture resembles fine bread-crumbs. Sprinkle the water over and mix, using a round-bladed knife, until the mixture begins to bind together to form a dough. Knead together very lightly and use as required.

Note: Throughout the recipes the above amount of pastry is referred to as 225 g/8 oz shortcrust pastry.

One-stage method

For quickness, an electric food mixer can be used. Place the flour and salt in a bowl, add the margarine, cut into small pieces, and sprinkle the water over. Mix using an electric mixer on the slowest speed, gradually increasing the speed as the mixture binds together. Knead lightly to form a dough and use as required.

Bought pastry

For even greater speed, buy chilled or frozen pastry, shortcrust or puff. Defrost frozen pastry at room temperature before use.

Baking 'blind'

This is the term used for par-baking an unfilled pastry shell to make sure it is well cooked, not limp and soggy, when served. Prick the pastry all over, then loosely line it with a piece of greaseproof paper and put in a handful of dried peas or beans, or baking beans. Bake in a moderately hot oven (200 C, 400 F, gas 6) for 15 minutes. The paper and peas will prevent the pastry from bubbling up during cooking; carefully remove them, add the filling and continue cooking according to the recipe instructions.

Wholemeal Shortcrust Pastry

225 g/8 oz wholemeal flour
pinch of salt
100 g/4 oz margarine
2 tablespoons cold water

Sift the flour and salt, into a mixing bowl and add the bran remaining in the sieve. Add the margarine and rub in lightly with the fingertips until the mixture resembles fine breadcrumbs.

Sprinkle the cold water over and mix with a round-bladed knife until the mixture begins to bind together, then finish off by gently kneading it to form a dough. Chill the pastry in the refrigerator until you want to use it. MAKES 225 g/8 oz

Sweet Flan Pastry

225 g/8 oz plain flour
175 g/6 oz butter
50 g/2 oz caster sugar
1 egg yolk

Sift the flour into a bowl. Rub in the butter with the fingertips until the mixture resembles fine breadcrumbs. Add the caster sugar and egg yolk. Mix with a round-bladed knife until the mixture binds together to form a dough. Knead lightly, and chill in the refrigerator until required. MAKES 225 g/8 oz

Flaky Pastry

(Illustrated on front cover)

175 g/6 oz lard
175 g/6 oz hard margarine
450 g/1 lb plain flour
$\frac{1}{2}$ teaspoon lemon juice
ice-cold water to mix

Mix the lard and margarine together until soft and divide into four equal portions. Sieve the flour into a bowl and rub in one quarter of the fat. Sprinkle over the lemon juice and water and, using a round-bladed knife, mix to an elastic dough.

Turn the dough out on to a floured surface and knead lightly, then roll out into an oblong and dot the second quarter of the fat over the top two-thirds of the pastry. Fold in three, placing the edge without fat over the centre and bringing the top down over the middle. Give the pastry a half turn and roll it out again, repeating the process until all the fat has been added. Finally roll out and fold once more before using. Chill for about 30 minutes if the pastry is slightly fatty (this may happen if the room is very warm). MAKES 450 g/1 lb

Variations on a Pastry Theme

Cheese Pastry

Variation on basic shortcrust recipe. Stir 50 g/2 oz finely grated mature Cheddar into the rubbed-in mixture before binding to a dough.

Savoury Shortcrust

Variation on basic shortcrust recipe. Finely crumble one chicken or beef-flavoured stock cube into the flour before rubbing in the fat.

Nut Pastry

Variation on basic shortcrust for savoury, or sweet flan pastry for sweet recipes. Replace 50 g/2 oz flour with 50 g/2 oz finely ground almonds or hazelnuts.

Lemon Pastry

Variation on basic shortcrust for savoury, or sweet flan pastry for sweet recipes. Stir the finely grated rind of one lemon into the rubbed-in mixture before binding to a dough.

Chocolate Pastry

Variation on sweet flan pastry. Replace 15 g/$\frac{1}{2}$ oz flour with 15 g/$\frac{1}{2}$ oz cocoa powder.

Herb Pastry

Variation on basic shortcrust recipe. Stir two teaspoons mixed herbs into the rubbed-in mixture before binding to a dough.

Marmite Pastry

Variation on basic shortcrust recipe. Blend one teaspoon Marmite or yeast extract with the water used to bind the rubbed-in mixture.

Cheesy Fish Pie

225 g/8 oz Cheese Pastry (opposite)
350 g/12 oz smoked haddock
350 g/12 oz cod or haddock
50 g/2 oz butter
1 small onion, chopped
100 g/4 oz button mushrooms
25 g/1 oz flour
300 ml/½ pint milk
100 g/4 oz frozen sweet corn
75 g/3 oz Cheddar cheese, grated
2 tablespoons chopped parsley
salt and freshly ground black pepper
beaten egg or milk to glaze

Make the pastry according to the recipe instructions and roll out to a circle or oval slightly larger than the top of a 1-litre/1¾-pint pie dish. Dampen the rim of the pie dish and line it with a strip of pastry trimmed from the edge.

Place the fish (both types) in a large saucepan and just cover with cold water. Bring slowly to the boil and simmer for 15–20 minutes. Drain, reserving 150 ml/¼ pint of the cooking liquor, and flake the fish, discarding the skin and bones.

Melt the butter in a saucepan, add the onion and mushrooms and cook gently until soft but not browned. Stir in the flour, gradually add the reserved stock and milk and bring to the boil, stirring continuously until the sauce is smooth and thick. Add the fish, sweet corn, cheese and parsley and season to taste. Pour the filling into the pie dish. Dampen the pastry rim with water, put the pastry lid on top and press the edges together. Use any trimmings to decorate the pie, then brush with beaten egg or milk. Bake in a moderately hot oven (200 C, 400 F, gas 6) for 30 minutes or until golden. SERVES 4–6

Crunchy Fish Finger Flan

(Illustrated on page 17)

225 g/8 oz Shortcrust Pastry (page 9)
225 g/8 oz cream cheese
1 egg, lightly beaten
4 spring onions, chopped
salt and pepper
3 tablespoons vegetable oil
6 frozen fish fingers
2 small tomatoes, sliced
25 g/1 oz Cheddar cheese, finely grated
2 tablespoons crushed potato crisps

Make the pastry according to the recipe instructions and use to line a 23-cm/9-in flan dish or loose-bottomed flan tin. Bake the flan blind in a moderately hot oven (200 C, 400 F, gas 6) for 15 minutes, then remove the paper and beans and continue to cook for a further 5 minutes.

Meanwhile prepare the filling. Blend the cream cheese until soft then stir in the egg and spring onions. Season well. Heat the oil in a frying pan and fry the fish fingers until crisp and golden, then drain on absorbent kitchen paper. Pour the cheese mixture into the bottom of the flan and spread over evenly. Arrange the fish fingers and tomato slices on top to look like the spokes of a wheel, then sprinkle with the grated cheese and crisps. Bake in a moderate oven (180 C, 350 F, gas 4) for 30–40 minutes or until set and golden brown. Serve hot with a crisp green salad and jacket potatoes. SERVES 6

Steak and Kidney Pie

575 g/1¼ lb lean braising or stewing steak
100 g/4 oz ox kidney
1 tablespoon plain flour
¼ teaspoon salt
¼ teaspoon pepper
1 medium onion
2 tablespoons beef dripping or oil
2 teaspoons Worcestershire sauce
300 ml/½ pint water
225 g/8 oz Shortcrust Pastry (page 9)

Cut the steak into 2.5-cm/1-in chunks and the kidney into slightly smaller pieces. Sift the flour with the salt and pepper and coat the pieces of meat well with the mixture. Chop the onion. Heat the dripping or oil in a pan, add the onion and meat and fry for about 2–3 minutes, until all the pieces of meat are sealed. Pour in the Worcestershire sauce and the water and bring to the boil, stirring continuously. Cover the pan and simmer the meat for 1¼– 2 hours, until tender. Stir from time to time to prevent the meat from sticking to the bottom of the pan.

Meanwhile, make the pastry according to the recipe instructions and roll it out to a circle slightly larger than a 900-ml/1½-pint pie dish. Put the meat into the dish with about half the gravy, reserving the rest. Cut a 1.5-cm/¾-in border from the pastry shape, dampen the rim of the pie dish and arrange the pastry strip all the way round, pressing down well. Now moisten the upper side of the pastry strip and place the remaining pastry shape on the pie, pressing the edges together with your finger and thumb to make a fluted pattern. Roll out any remaining pastry and use it to cut out leaves and other decorations for the top of the pie, then brush the pie with beaten egg.

Bake in a hot oven (220 C, 425 F, gas 7) for 15–20 minutes to set the pastry, then lower the heat to 190 C, 375 F, gas 5 and cook for a further 20 minutes. Heat the reserved gravy in a pan and serve it in a sauce boat with the pie. SERVES 4–6

Picnic Pie

(Illustrated opposite)

225 g/8 oz Wholemeal Shortcrust Pastry (page 10)
350 g/12 oz pork sausagemeat
1 small onion, finely chopped
3 tablespoons fresh white breadcrumbs
1 teaspoon dried mixed herbs
2 hard-boiled eggs, shelled
beaten egg or milk to glaze

Make the pastry according to the recipe instructions. Roll out two-thirds of it on a lightly floured surface and use to line a 450-g/1-lb loaf tin.

Prepare the filling by mixing the sausagemeat, onion, breadcrumbs and herbs together. Place half this mixture in the base of the tin. Arrange the two hard-boiled eggs along the centre and cover with the remaining sausagemeat mixture.

Roll out the remaining pastry to form a lid. Dampen the edge of the pastry with water and cover the pie with the pastry lid. Trim and flute the edges, and use any pastry trimmings to make leaves to decorate the top of the pie. Make a small hole in the centre to allow any steam to escape. Brush with beaten egg or milk.

Cook in a moderately hot oven (190 C, 375 F, gas 5) for 1 hour or until cooked. Serve cold with salad. SERVES 6

Picnic Pie and Crunchy Fish Finger Flan (page 14)

Beany Pie

225 g/8 oz Savoury Shortcrust Pastry (page 12)
1 green pepper (optional)
2 tablespoons vegetable oil
1 onion, chopped
1 (340-g/12-oz) can corned beef
1 (450-g/15.9-oz) can baked beans
1 teaspoon horseradish sauce
salt and pepper
beaten egg or milk to glaze

Make the pastry according to the recipe instructions and roll out to a rough circle slightly larger than the top of a 1-litre/1¾-pint pie dish. Dampen the rim of the dish and line it with a strip of pastry cut from the edge.

Cut the stalk end off the pepper, if using, remove all the seeds and pith, then chop the flesh. Heat the oil in a frying pan, add the onion and green pepper and cook until the vegetables are soft but not browned. Roughly break up the corned beef with a fork and add it to the pan together with the baked beans and horseradish sauce. Season lightly, bearing in mind that the baked beans and corned beef are already seasoned. Pour the filling into the pie dish. Dampen the pastry rim with water, put the pastry circle on top and press together. Use any trimmings to decorate the pie, then brush with beaten egg or milk. Bake in a moderately hot oven (200 C, 400 F, gas 6) for 30 minutes or until golden brown. Serve immediately. SERVES 4

Almond and Apple Flan (page 28) and Lemon Meringue Pie (page 27)

Cowboy Turnovers

225 g/8 oz Shortcrust Pastry (page 9)
2 tablespoons vegetable oil
4 frozen beefburgers, thawed
1 small onion, chopped
1 (225-g/7.94-oz) can baked beans
2 teaspoons black treacle
1 teaspoon Worcestershire sauce
2 teaspoons tomato ketchup
salt and freshly ground black pepper
beaten egg to glaze

Make the pastry according to the recipe instructions and divide into eight portions. Roll out each portion into a 15-cm/6-in round using a saucer as a guide. Heat the oil in a frying pan and fry the beefburgers gently for about 3 minutes on each side. Remove from the pan and drain on absorbent kitchen paper. Fry the onion in the remaining oil until soft but not browned. Drain off any excess oil, stir in the baked beans, black treacle, Worcestershire sauce and tomato ketchup, and season to taste.

Place a spoonful of bean mixture on each pastry circle. Halve the beefburgers and place on top of the beans, then spoon over the remaining bean mixture. Glaze the edge of the pastry with beaten egg, then fold one side of the pastry over the filling to form a semi-circle. Seal and crimp the edges and use any pastry trimmings cut into initials to decorate the turnovers. Arrange on a greased baking tray and glaze with the remaining beaten egg. Bake in a moderately hot oven (200 C, 400 F, gas 6) for 30 minutes or until golden brown. MAKES 8

Cornish Pasties

225 g/8 oz Shortcrust Pastry (page 9)
225 g/8 oz braising steak
1 carrot
1 medium potato
1 medium onion, chopped
2 tablespoons beef stock
salt and freshly ground black pepper
2 tablespoons chopped parsley
beaten egg or milk to glaze

Grease a baking tray. Make the pastry according to the recipe instructions. Cut the meat into small cubes and dice the carrot and potato. Mix the meat and vegetables with the stock and season generously. Stir in the chopped parsley.

Divide the pastry into four pieces and roll each piece out to a 15-cm/6-in circle. Divide the meat mixture between the pastry circles and dampen the edges with water. Bring the edges together over the middle of the filling and seal to form an enclosed pasty. Place on the baking tray and brush with a little beaten egg or milk then bake in a moderately hot oven (200 C, 400 F, gas 6) for 15 minutes. Reduce the temperature to moderate (180 C, 350 F, gas 4) and cook for a further 50–60 minutes. Serve hot or cold. MAKES 4

———————— FREEZER TO MICROWAVE ————————

Wrap the pasties individually in freezer film, label each one with a large label showing reheating instructions. Place the pasties on a baking tray and freeze; when hard, pack them all in one bag. From frozen, on full power in the microwave oven, one pasty will be hot in 3 minutes. Older children will cheerfully reheat their own pasties for supper.

On the label
Cornish Pasty/Date
Unwrap, put on plate
Microwave: 3 minutes on full power

Scotch Pasties

(Illustrated on pages 134/135)

450 g/1 lb pork sausagemeat
2 tablespoons chopped parsley
4 hard-boiled eggs
1 (212-g/7½-oz) packet frozen puff pastry, thawed
1 egg, beaten
oil for deep frying

Mix the sausagemeat with the parsley and divide into four equal portions. Shell the eggs and place one on top of each portion of sausagemeat. Mould the meat mixture evenly around each egg to coat it completely. Roll out the pastry on a lightly floured board and cut out four circles slightly larger than the sausage-covered eggs. Brush with beaten egg and place one egg on each circle, carefully folding the pastry around and sealing the edges well.

Heat the oil to 180 C/350 F or until a cube of day-old bread turns golden in 1 minute. Deep fry the scotch pasties for 4–5 minutes or until golden brown. Drain on absorbent kitchen paper and serve at once. MAKES 4

Pork and Apple Pasties

225 g/8 oz Shortcrust Pastry (page 9)
350 g/12 oz lean pork
1 cooking apple
1 onion, chopped
½ teaspoon sage
2 tablespoons dry cider or chicken stock
salt and freshly ground black pepper
beaten egg or milk to glaze

Grease a baking tray. Make the pastry according to the recipe instructions. Cut the pork into small cubes. Peel, core and finely dice the apple, mix with the pork, onion, sage and cider, and season to taste.

Divide the pastry into four pieces and roll each piece out to a 15-cm/6-in circle using a saucer as a guide. Divide the meat mixture between the circles, dampen the edges with water and bring together over the middle of the filling. Seal and pleat the edges and place the pasties on the prepared baking tray. Brush with a little beaten egg or milk and bake in a moderately hot oven (200 C, 400 F, gas 6) for 15 minutes then reduce the oven temperature to moderate (180 C, 350 F, gas 4) and bake for a further 50–60 minutes. Serve hot. MAKES 4

Chicken and Sausage Pie

225 g/8 oz Shortcrust Pastry (page 9)
225 g/8 oz boneless chicken breast
2 tablespoons vegetable oil
225 g/8 oz pork cocktail sausages
1 onion, chopped
2 tablespoons flour
300 ml/$\frac{1}{2}$ pint chicken stock
2 teaspoons soy sauce
grated rind of $\frac{1}{2}$ lemon
2 tablespoons chopped parsley
1 (184-g/6$\frac{1}{2}$-oz) can sweet red peppers, drained
1 (198-g/7-oz) can sweet corn, drained
salt and freshly ground pepper
beaten egg or milk to glaze

Make the pastry according to the recipe instructions and roll out to a circle slightly larger than the top of a 600-ml/1-pint pie dish. Dampen the rim of the dish and line it with a strip of pastry cut from the edge of the rolled piece.

Cut the chicken into bite-sized pieces. Heat the oil in a frying pan and cook the chicken until lightly browned. Remove from the pan with a slotted spoon and keep on one side. Add the sausages to the pan and fry until golden brown. Remove from the pan and keep on one side with the chicken. Fry the onion in the remaining oil until soft but not browned. Stir in the flour, gradually add the stock and bring to the boil, stirring continuously until the sauce is smooth and thick. Return the chicken and sausages to the sauce together with the remaining ingredients. Season to taste.

Pour the filling into the pie dish. Dampen the pastry rim with water, top with the rolled pastry, and use any trimmings to decorate the pie. Brush with beaten egg or milk. Bake in a moderately hot oven (200 C, 400 F, gas 6) for 30 minutes or until golden. Serve immediately. Serves 4

Golden Flan

225 g/8 oz Cheese Pastry (page 12)
1 (298-g/10½-oz) can creamed sweet corn
3 eggs, lightly beaten
75 g/3 oz carrots, grated
100 g/4 oz Cheddar cheese, grated
salt and freshly ground pepper

Make the pastry according to the recipe instructions and use to line a 23-cm/9-in flan tin. Bake the flan blind in a moderately hot oven (200 C, 400 F, gas 6) for 15 minutes then remove the paper and beans and cook for a further 5 minutes.

Meanwhile prepare the filling. Mix together the sweet corn, eggs, carrots and cheese, season well, and pour into the flan case. Bake in a moderate oven (180 C, 350 F, gas 4) for 30–40 minutes or until set and golden brown. Serves 6

_____ Freezer to Microwave _____

Wrap individual slices of flan in freezer film, label and place on a baking tray. When hard, pack in one bag. From frozen, on full power in the microwave oven, one slice will be hot in 1½–2 minutes. Good with salad for Dad or with baked beans for younger members of the family.

On the label
Golden Flan / Date
Unwrap, put on plate
Microwave: 1½–2 minutes on full power

Liver and Bacon Triangles

1 (212-g/7½-oz) packet frozen puff pastry, thawed
25 g/1 oz butter
1 small onion, finely chopped
225 g/8 oz lean bacon, rind removed and finely chopped
225 g/8 oz lambs' liver, trimmed and finely chopped
1 teaspoon sage
salt and freshly ground black pepper
beaten egg or milk to glaze

Roll out the pastry and cut it into four 20-cm/8-in squares. Melt the butter in a frying pan, add the onion and cook until the onion is soft but not browned. Add the bacon and liver and continue to cook, stirring continuously, until the liver has changed colour. Add the sage and season well. Leave to cool.

Place a quarter of the filling on each of the pastry squares and dampen the edges with water. Fold one side of the pastry over the filling to form a triangle. Brush with beaten egg or milk and place on a dampened baking tray. Bake in a moderately hot oven (200 C, 400 F, gas 6) for 20–30 minutes until well puffed and golden brown. MAKES 4

Lemon Meringue Pie

(Illustrated on page 18)

1 quantity shortcrust pastry (page 9)
1 (397-g/14-oz) can condensed milk
grated rind and juice of 1 lemon
2 eggs, separated
2 teaspoons cream of tartare
50 g/2 oz caster sugar
glaće cherries, quartered, to decorate

Make the pastry following the recipe instructions then roll it out and use to line a 23-cm/9-in flan dish. Bake blind in a moderately hot oven (190 C, 375 F, gas 5) for 20 minutes.

Mix the condensed milk , lemon rind and juice, egg yolks and cream of tartare, then pour this mixture into the flan case. Whisk the egg whites until stiff, then fold in half the sugar. Pile or pipe the meringue all over the filled flan. Sprinkle the remaining sugar over the top and decorate with the cherries.

Bake in a very cool oven (110 C, 225 F, gas $\frac{1}{4}$) for 1$\frac{1}{2}$ to 2 hours or until the meringue is dry. Alternatively put the meringue in a moderately hot oven (200 C, 400 F, gas 6) for 10 – 12 minutes, or until golden. Allow to cool before serving. SERVES 6

Note: If you like the pastry can be used to line individual tartlet tins, or patty tins to make small lemon meringue pies.

Almond and Apple Flan

(Illustrated on page 18)

450 g/1 lb Nut Pastry (page 12)
1 kg/2 lb cooking apples
grated rind and juice of 1 lemon
125 g/4½ oz sugar
1 teaspoon cinnamon
100 g/4 oz raisins
100 g/4 oz blanched almonds, chopped
1 egg yolk, beaten, to glaze

Make the pastry according to the recipe instructions. Peel the apples, chop roughly and mix with the lemon rind and juice, sugar, cinnamon, raisins and almonds. Roll out three-quarters of the pastry and use it to line the base and sides of a 23×33-cm/ 9×13-in Swiss roll tin. Spread the apple mixture over the pastry. Roll out the remaining pastry, cut into thin strips and arrange over the flan in a lattice pattern. Brush with beaten egg yolk and bake the flan for 30–40 minutes in a moderately hot oven (200 C, 400 F, gas 6). Leave to cool, then serve with cream or ice cream. SERVES 8

Banana Flan

225 g/8 oz Sweet Flan Pastry (page 10)
2 tablespoons custard powder · 1 tablespoon sugar
300 ml/½ pint milk · 2 large bananas
100 g/4 oz marshmallows

Make the pastry according to the recipe instructions and use to line a 23-cm/9-in flan tin. Bake the flan blind (see page 9) in a moderately hot oven (200 C, 400 F, gas 6) for 15 minutes, remove the paper or foil and beans and continue to cook for a further 15–20 minutes or until cooked.

Meanwhile make the filling. Blend the custard powder and sugar with 4 tablespoons milk. Bring the remaining milk to the boil and pour quickly onto the custard mixture. Stir well and return to the saucepan. Bring to the boil, stirring continuously, and continue to cook for 1–2 minutes. Slice the bananas and place in the bottom of the flan case. Pour over the custard and arrange the marshmallows on top. Bake in a moderate oven (180 C, 350 F, gas 4) for about 5 minutes or until the marshmallows have melted. SERVES 6

Apple Parcels

225 g/8 oz Sweet Flan Pastry (page 10)
4 small cooking apples · 8 tablespoons strawberry jam
a little milk · caster sugar for sprinkling

Make the pastry according to the recipe instructions and roll it out into four circles, each large enough to enclose an apple. Peel and core the cooking apples. Place one apple on each circle of pastry, and spoon the jam into the middle of each one. Dampen the edges of the pastry and fold it up around the fruit. Trim off any excess pastry and use as decoration. Seal the edges and place the dumplings sealed side down on a greased baking tray.

Brush lightly with milk and sprinkle a little sugar over. Make a small hole in the top of each dumpling and bake in a moderately hot oven (200 C, 400 F, gas 6) for 30 minutes. SERVES 4

Packed School Lunches

Making a packed lunch taste more interesting is a continuing battle but it is important that the children eat their lunch and that they enjoy it too. It is also quite likely that Dad would appreciate an occasional break from boring old sandwiches.

If you do ever have the time, then this chapter offers a few ideas for turning packet bread mix into interesting rolls and there is a recipe for cheese scones. Remember that you can make a large batch of these items and store them in the freezer.

To make a complete change why not try making some savoury individual quiches, sausage rolls or a Savoury Lunch Box Slice? Sweet things have not been forgotten but remember to include some fruit (an apple or banana are less messy than an orange) or a carton of yogurt in the lunch pack. A small flask of hot soup or drinking chocolate is also welcome on a cold day.

Bread Mix Rolls

These recipes are all based on packets of bread mix, and show you different ways to shape and flavour them. Each one uses a 567-g/ 1 lb 4-oz packet of white or brown bread mix.

Cottage Rolls

Divide the dough into 16 pieces. Taking each piece in turn, cut off one-third and knead both pieces into rounds. Place the larger round on the greased baking tray. Brush the top with water and place the smaller round on top. Push a floured finger down the centre of both rounds to fix them firmly together. Bake according to packet instructions.

Bridge Rolls

Divide the dough into 24 pieces. Knead each piece of dough and roll into a thin sausage shape about 7.5 cm/3 in long, slightly tapering off at the ends. Place the rolls close together on the greased baking tray and bake according to packet instructions.

Clover Leaf Rolls

Divide the dough into 16 pieces and then divide each piece into three parts and shape into small balls. Place on the greased baking tray in the form of a clover leaf, pressing lightly together. Bake according to packet instructions.

Twists and Knots

Divide the dough into 16 pieces and, using both hands, roll each piece into a long sausage. Tie in knots or twist into figures-of-eight. Bake according to packet instructions.

Scones

These freeze well and make an excellent addition to a lunch box meal. The Cheese Scones taste good filled with some of the sandwich fillings.

225 g/8 oz self-raising flour
pinch of salt
1 teaspoon baking powder
50 g/2 oz margarine or butter
2 tablespoons caster sugar
scant 150 ml/¼ pint milk plus extra for glazing

Sift the flour, salt and baking powder into a bowl. Add the fat, cut into pieces, and rub it in with your fingertips until the mixture resembles fine breadcrumbs. Stir in the sugar and gradually add the milk to make a soft dough. Turn this out on to a floured surface and knead together very lightly, then roll out to 1-cm/½-in thick.

Cut out 5–7.5-cm/2–3-in circles and place them on a greased baking tray. Glaze with a little milk and bake in a hot oven (220 C, 425 F, gas 7) for 12–15 minutes, until well risen and golden. Cool on a wire rack. Makes 12–16 (depending on size).

Fruit Scones

Add 50 g/2 oz sultanas to the dry ingredients. Continue as above.

Cheese Scones

Omit the sugar in the above recipe. Add 50 g/2 oz finely grated strong Cheddar cheese to the dry ingredients. Continue as above.

Fillings for Rolls and Sandwiches

It's too easy to get into a rut with packed school lunches, so here is a selection of tempting fillings to keep the children interested.

Corned Beef and Egg (*Illustrated on page 36*)

Line four halved and buttered crusty rolls with lettuce. Mash a 198-g/7-oz can of corned beef with one tablespoon horseradish sauce and one tablespoon tomato sauce, spoon this mixture over the lettuce. Finally arrange two or three slices of hard-boiled egg and a gherkin fan over the corned beef.

Peanut Butter and Crispy Bacon

Thinly spread eight slices of bread with butter then spread thickly with crunchy peanut butter. Grill twelve rashers of rindless streaky bacon until crisp. Slice four tomatoes and arrange on four slices of bread. Top with the bacon and remaining bread.

Pineapple and Curd Cheese

Thinly spread eight slices of Granary bread with butter. Drain and chop a 205-g/7.1-oz can of pineapple rings and blend with 225 g/8 oz cream cheese. Sprinkle a little cress over four slices of bread, then top with the cheese and remaining bread.

Coleslaw and Frankfurter Sausage

Thinly spread eight slices of bread with butter. Spoon a little homemade coleslaw over four slices and top with thickly sliced Frankfurters and the remaining slices of bread.

Sardine and Cucumber

Mash a can of sardines in tomato sauce with a little black pepper then stir in 50 g/2 oz finely diced cucumber. Use as a filling for eight slices of buttered bread.

Cream Cheese and Dates

Warm 100 g/4 oz cooking dates under a low grill for a minute or two, then chop them finely. Mix with 225 g/8 oz cream cheese and 50 g/2 oz chopped walnuts, then use to fill eight slices of buttered Granary bread.

Savoury Lunch-Break Slice

(Illustrated opposite)

1 (567-g/1 lb 4-oz) packet bread mix
2 tablespoons oil
1 medium onion, chopped
225 g/8 oz minced beef
100 g/4 oz carrots, grated
100 g/4 oz frozen peas
1 (397-g/14-oz) can tomatoes
4 tablespoons tomato purée
3 eggs, lightly beaten
salt and black pepper

Lightly grease a 23×33-cm/9×13-in Swiss roll tin.

Make up the bread mix according to packet instructions and use two-thirds of the dough to line the Swiss roll tin. The best way to do this is to stretch the dough over your hands, then to press it neatly into the tin and up the sides. Cover with lightly oiled cling film and leave in a warm place to rise for 15 minutes.

Meanwhile prepare the filling. Heat the oil in a frying pan and fry the onion until soft but not brown. Add the minced beef and continue to cook for a further 5 minutes. Add the carrots, peas, tomatoes with their juice, and the tomato purée and cook for another 10 minutes. Leave to cool slightly and then add the eggs, keeping a little aside for glazing. Season to taste.

Fill the lined Swiss roll tin with the meat mixture. Roll out the remaining dough to form a lid, cover with oiled cling film and leave in a warm place to rise for 15 minutes. Glaze with beaten egg and bake in a moderately hot oven (200 C, 400 F, gas 6) for 30–40 minutes until golden brown. SERVES 4

A packed school lunch: a piece of Savoury Lunch-break Slice, a slice of Quick Apple Cake (page 43) with sticks of celery and carrot, a carton of yogurt, an apple, orange and a few sweets.

STEVEN COLLINS

tte mallette appartient à
ieser koffer gehört
is lunch box belongs to

18'm G

1 sunday   dimanche

   Monday   lundi

     Tuesday   mardi

                            ercredi

INDIVIDUAL QUICHES

These tasty tartlets with quiche-like fillings are baked in bun tins and are ideal for the lunch box.

Cheese Quiches

(Illustrated opposite)

175 g/6 oz Shortcrust Pastry (page 9)
2 tablespoons oil
1 medium onion, finely chopped
2 eggs
3 tablespoons milk
salt and black pepper
100 g/4 oz Cheddar cheese, grated

Make the pastry according to the recipe instructions and use to line 12 patty tins. Bake the pastry cases blind in a moderately hot oven (200 C, 400 F, gas 6) for 10 minutes then remove the paper or foil and beans and continue to cook for a further 5 minutes.

Heat the oil in a pan and fry the onion until soft but not brown. Beat the eggs lightly and add the milk, seasoning, cheese and onion. Fill the pastry cases with the mixture and bake in a moderately hot oven (200 C, 400 F, gas 6) for 15–20 minutes until lightly browned and set. Leave the quiches to cool before removing them from the patty tins. MAKES 12

A packed school lunch: a Corned Beef and Egg Roll (page 33), a couple of slices of Spiced Banana Bread (page 42), a Cheese Quiche and Chicken and Ham Quiches (page 38) with hot tomato soup and an apple.

Chicken and Ham Quiches

(Illustrated on page 36)

175 g/6 oz Shortcrust Pastry (page 9)
40 g/1½ oz butter or margarine
1 small onion, finely chopped
50 g/2 oz button mushrooms, sliced
65 g/2½ oz plain flour · 250 ml/8 fl oz milk
100 g/4 oz cooked chicken meat, cubed
50 g/2 oz cooked ham, diced · salt and black pepper
100 g/4 oz Cheddar cheese, finely grated
50 g/2 oz breadcrumbs

Make the pastry according to the recipe instructions and use to line 12 patty tins. Bake the pastry cases blind in a moderately hot oven (200 C, 400 F, gas 6) for 10 minutes, then remove the paper and beans and continue to cook for a further 5 minutes.

Melt the butter in a frying pan, add the onion and cook until soft but not brown. Add the sliced mushrooms and cook for a further 1 minute then sprinkle the flour over and cook gently for a few minutes more. Gradually pour in the milk, stirring continuously, and bring the mixture to the boil. Cook for about 1 minute, still stirring, until the sauce thickens, and then add the chicken, ham and seasoning.

Fill the pastry cases with the mixture and sprinkle with the grated cheese and breadcrumbs. Bake for 15–20 minutes until golden brown and set. Leave the quiches to cool before removing them from the patty tins. Makes 12

———————— Freezer to Microwave ————————

These little quiches are also good served as teatime fillers. Freeze the cooked quiches on a baking tray, then individually wrap and label them. From frozen, on full power in the microwave oven, one quiche will be hot in ¾–1 minute.

On the label
Chicken and Ham Quiche/Date
Unwrap, put on plate
Microwave: ¾–1 minute on full power

Corned Beef Quiches

175 g/6 oz Shortcrust Pastry (page 9)
1 (198-g/7-oz) can corned beef
1 small onion
2 tablespoons oil
2 tablespoons plain flour
6 tablespoons tomato sauce
1 (46-g/1.62-oz) packet minestrone soup
made up with 300 ml/½ pint water
salt and black pepper

Make the pastry according to the recipe instructions and use this to line 12 patty tins. Bake the pastry cases blind in a moderately hot oven (200 C, 400 F, gas 6) for 10 minutes then remove the paper and beans and continue to cook for a further 5 minutes.

Meanwhile prepare the filling. Cut the corned beef into small cubes, and finely chop the onion. Heat the oil in a frying pan and fry the onion until soft but not browned, add the flour to make a paste, then add the tomato sauce, corned beef, minestrone soup and seasoning.

Fill the pastry cases with the mixture and bake in a moderately hot oven (200 C, 400 F, gas 6) for 15–20 minutes until set. Leave the quiches to cool before removing them from the patty tins.
MAKES 12

Cheesy Sausage Rolls

(Illustrated on front cover)

225 g/8 oz Wholemeal Shortcrust Pastry (page 10) *or* 255 g/8 oz
Flaky Pastry (page 11) *or* 1 (212-g/7½-oz) packet frozen
puff pastry, thawed
50–75 g/2–3 oz mature Cheddar or other strong cheese, grated
450 g/1 lb premium pork sausagemeat · beaten egg to glaze

Roll out the pastry to a rectangle 25 × 50 cm/10 × 20 in and sprinkle
with the cheese. Fold into three, bringing the top third over the
centre and folding the bottom up over both layers. Seal the edges
with the rolling pin. Leave to chill for about 20–30 minutes. Roll
out the pastry again to the original-sized rectangle and cut it in
half lengthways. Form the sausagemeat into two rolls and lay one
down the middle of each piece of pastry. Dampen the edges of
the pastry and turn it over to seal in the meat. Brush with the egg.
Cut the long rolls into smaller bite-sized ones, making two cuts
on top of each. Bake in a hot oven (220C, 425F, gas 7) for 20–25
minutes until golden brown. MAKES ABOUT 16–18

VARIATIONS ON THE SAUSAGE ROLL

Savoury Sausage Rolls

1 small onion · 4 rashers rindless streaky bacon
225 g/8 oz pork sausagemeat · 3 tablespoons brown sauce
1 egg, lightly beaten
1 (212-g/7½-oz) packet frozen puff pastry, thawed

Finely chop the onion and bacon and mix together with the
sausagemeat, brown sauce and half the beaten egg.
   Roll out the pastry on a lightly floured surface to a rectangle
measuring 20 × 30 cm/8 × 12 in and cut it in half lengthways.
   Divide the sausage mixture in half and arrange down the
middle of each piece of pastry. Dampen the edges of the pastry

and fold it over the sausage mixture, pressing the edges together, and brush with the remaining beaten egg. Now divide both pieces into quarters and bake in a hot oven (220C, 425F, gas 7) for 15–20 minutes until risen and golden brown. MAKES 8

Cheesy Sausage Spirals

(Illustrated on pages 134/135)

100 g/4 oz Edam cheese
450 g/1 lb pork sausagemeat
1 (212-g/7½-oz) packet frozen puff pastry, thawed
½ beaten egg to glaze

Cut the cheese into eight 7.5-cm/3-in strips. Divide the sausage-meat into eight and mould each portion around a strip of cheese to form a sausage shape.

Roll out the pastry on a lightly floured surface to a rectangle measuring 15×30 cm/6×12 in, then cut into eight 1·5-cm/¾-in strips. Wind the strips around the sausage shapes to form a spiral, and brush with beaten egg. Bake in a hot oven (220C, 425F, gas 7) for 15–20 minutes until golden brown. MAKES 8

Peanut Butter Sausage Rolls

1 (212-g/7½-oz) packet frozen puff pastry, thawed
2 tablespoons crunchy peanut butter
225 g/8 oz pork sausagemeat · ½ beaten egg to glaze

Roll out pastry on a lightly floured surface to a rectangle measuring 20×30 cm/8×12 in. Cut the pastry in half lengthways and spread with peanut butter, leaving a 1-cm/½-in border at the edge.

Divide the sausagemeat in half and arrange down the middle of each pastry half. Dampen the edges with water and fold the pastry over the sausagemeat. Press the edges together and brush with beaten egg. Now divide each half into four and bake in a hot oven (220C, 425F, gas 7) for 15–20 minutes until the sausage rolls are well risen and golden brown. MAKES 8

Spiced Banana Bread

(Illustrated on page 36)

225 g/8 oz self-raising flour
1 teaspoon mixed spice
½ teaspoon cinnamon · ¼ teaspoon salt
50 g/2 oz margarine · 50 g/2 oz caster sugar
50 g/2 oz brazil nuts, chopped
75 g/3 oz sultanas · 2 bananas
75 g/3 oz golden syrup · 1 egg

Grease a large (1-kg/2-lb) loaf tin. Sift the flour, spices and salt into a bowl, rub in the margarine with your fingers until the mixture resembles fine breadcrumbs and then add the caster sugar, chopped nuts and sultanas. Mash the bananas with the golden syrup, and then beat in the egg. Stir the banana mixture into the dry ingredients and mix well together.

Turn into the prepared loaf tin and bake in the centre of a moderate oven (180C, 350F, gas 4) for about 1 hour. Cool in the tin and when cold turn out and serve sliced with butter.
Makes about 12 slices

Cinnamon Biscuits

225 g/8 oz self-raising flour · 2 teaspoons cinnamon
100 g/4 oz margarine · 100 g/4 oz caster sugar
1 egg, beaten · 25 g/1 oz blanched almonds

Sift the flour and cinnamon together, then cream the margarine and sugar together until light and fluffy. Work in the egg and finally the sifted flour.

Roll out thinly and cut into rounds. Split each of the almonds and put half on each biscuit. Place on a greased baking tray and bake in a moderate oven (180C, 350F, gas 4) for 10 minutes. Lift off carefully and cool on a wire rack. Makes about 24

Quick Apple Cake

(Illustrated on page 35)

1 (326-g/11½-oz) packet plain sponge cake mix
4–5 dessert apples · juice of 1 lemon
2 tablespoons raisins
3 tablespoons apple jelly or apricot jam

Grease a 25-cm/10-in springform cake tin. Make up the cake mix according to the packet instructions and turn into the tin. Spread the top smoothly.

Peel the apples, quarter them and remove the cores. Cut into thin slices in the lemon juice. Sprinkle half the raisins over the cake and arrange the apple slices thickly in a rosette shape on top. Sprinkle with the rest of the raisins and bake for 25–30 minutes in a moderately hot oven (200C, 400F, gas 6).

Warm the apple jelly or apricot jam, stirring all the time, and brush over the apples while they are still hot. SERVES 6

Fruity Biscuits

100 g/4 oz self-raising flour
100 g/4 oz fine semolina
100 g/4 oz butter · 100 g/4 oz caster sugar
grated rind of 1 orange · 100 g/4 oz currants
1 egg, beaten · 1 tablespoon milk

Sift the flour and semolina together, then rub in the butter until the mixture is like fine breadcrumbs. Stir in the sugar, orange rind and currants. Whisk the egg and milk together and work into the dry mixture to make a stiff but light dough.

Roll out thinly and cut into large rounds using a biscuit cutter or the rim of a glass. Place the biscuits on greased baking trays and cook in a moderate oven (180C, 350F, gas 4) for 10–12 minutes. Cool on a wire rack. MAKES ABOUT 24

After-school Tea

The minute most children arrive home from school their hunger comes to the fore and they will dive for the biscuit tin if tea preparations are not very much in evidence!

Savoury bakes and some fresh salad ingredients are often the best fillers – quiches, pizzas and tasty turnovers would go down well with tomatoes, cucumber, apple and celery for example. Follow up with a slice of teabread or a piece of cake and the family will be ready to face the last lap of the day whether it's spent out on the tennis court, sitting at the piano or frowning over the latest batch of homework.

Variations on Pizza Squares

Chequer-board Pizzas

$\frac{1}{2}$ (567-g/1 lb 4-oz) packet white bread mix
2 tablespoons vegetable oil
Tomato topping
1 large onion, chopped
1 clove garlic, crushed
1 (397-g/14-oz) can chopped tomatoes
2 tablespoons tomato purée
1 teaspoon basil
1 teaspoon oregano
2 bay leaves
pinch of sugar
salt and freshly ground black pepper
To finish
50 g/2 oz Cheddar cheese
50 g/2 oz Red Leicester cheese

Lightly grease an 18×28-cm/7×11-in baking tray. Prepare the bread mix according to the packet instructions, halving the quantity of liquid, and use to line the tray, then brush all over with one tablespoon of the oil and leave in a warm place until the dough has risen to double its size.

Meanwhile make the tomato topping. Heat the remaining oil in a saucepan and gently cook the onion until soft but not browned. Add the garlic and fry for a further minute then stir in the tomatoes with their juice, tomato purée, herbs and sugar, and season well. Bring to the boil and simmer gently, stirring occasionally, for 20 minutes. Spread evenly over the bread dough. Slice the cheeses into neat, even squares and arrange in a chequer-board fashion on top of the tomato mixture. Bake in a hot oven (220C, 425F, gas7) for 20–25 minutes or until risen and lightly browned. Serve cut into squares, with salads.
Makes 9 pieces

Wiggly Bacon Pizzas

(Illustrated on page 54)

½ (567-g/1 lb 4-oz) packet white bread mix
2 tablespoons vegetable oil
1 quantity Tomato topping (see Chequer-board Pizzas)
100 g/4 oz button mushrooms, sliced
225 g/8 oz rindless streaky bacon
1 (120-g/4½-oz) packet Mozzarella cheese
1 tablespoon chopped parsley

Lightly grease an 18×28-cm/7×11-in baking tray. Prepare the bread mix according to the packet instructions, halving the quantity of liquid, and use to line the prepared tray, then brush all over with one tablespoon of the oil and leave in a warm place until the dough has risen to double its size.

Meanwhile, prepare the tomato topping according to the instructions in the previous recipe. Heat the remaining tablespoon of oil in a frying pan and cook the mushrooms until soft but not browned. Twist the bacon rashers firmly into spirals and thinly slice the Mozzarella cheese.

Spread the tomato topping evenly over the bread dough. Lay the bacon on top keeping the rashers well twisted and arrange the mushrooms over them. Sprinkle with parsley and cheese, then bake in a hot oven (220C, 425F, gas 7) for 20–25 minutes or until risen and lightly browned. Serve cut into squares, with salads.

MAKES 9 PIECES

———————— FREEZER TO MICROWAVE ————————

Individually wrap and label the cooled pizza squares, then pack them all in one bag. From frozen, on full power in the microwave oven, one piece will be hot in 2 minutes.

On the label
Wiggly Bacon Pizzas/Date
Unwrap, put on plate
Microwave: 2 minutes on full power

Salami and Pepper Pizzas

½ (567-g/1 lb 4-oz) packet white bread mix
2 tablespoons vegetable oil
1 quantity Tomato topping (see Chequer-board Pizzas)
½ red pepper
½ green pepper
or 1 large red or green pepper
1 (120-g/4½-oz) packet Mozzarella cheese
75 g/3 oz German or Hungarian salami

Lightly grease an 18×28-cm/7×11-in baking tray. Prepare the
bread mix according to the packet instructions, halving the
quantity of liquid, then use to line the prepared tray; brush all
over with one tablespoon of the oil and leave in a warm place until
the dough has risen to double its size.

Meanwhile prepare the tomato topping according to the recipe
for Chequer-board Pizzas. Cut the stalk end off the peppers,
remove all the seeds and pith then cut the flesh into strips. Heat
the remaining tablespoon of oil in a frying pan, add the peppers
and cook for 1–2 minutes or until they begin to soften. Remove
from the pan with a slotted spoon and drain on absorbent kitchen
paper.

Spread the tomato topping evenly over the bread dough.
Thinly slice the cheese and cover the tomato with it, then arrange
the salami and peppers diagonally on top.

Bake in a hot oven (220 C, 425 F, gas 7) for 20–25 minutes or until
risen and lightly browned. Serve cut into squares, with salads.
MAKES 9 PIECES

Hot Dog Rolls

(Illustrated on page 133)

1 (212-g/7½-oz) packet frozen puff pastry, thawed
1 tablespoon vegetable oil
1 small onion, finely chopped
2 tablespoons tomato ketchup
1 teaspoon wholegrain mustard
salt and freshly ground black pepper
6 Frankfurter sausages · beaten egg to glaze

Lightly grease a baking tray. Roll out the pastry to a 25×30-cm/ 10×12-in rectangle and cut into six 13×10-cm/5×4-in rectangles.

Heat the oil in a frying pan and cook the onion until golden brown. Mix together the tomato ketchup, mustard and onion. Season to taste. Divide the onion mixture between the pastry rectangles and spread out evenly, leaving a 1-cm/½-in border all round.

Place a Frankfurter sausage on top, brush the pastry border with a little beaten egg and wrap it over, sealing the edges well. Arrange on the prepared baking tray and make diagonal slashes down the centre of each roll, glazing with beaten egg. Bake in a hot oven (220C, 425F, gas7) for about 20 minutes or until well risen and golden brown. MAKES 6

Tuna-time Envelopes

(Illustrated on page 53)

1 (212-g/7½-oz) packet frozen puff pastry, thawed
25 g/1 oz butter · 1 medium onion, finely chopped
100 g/4 oz mushrooms, sliced
1 (198-g/7-oz) can sweet corn kernels, drained
1 (198-g/7-oz) can tuna, drained and flaked
beaten egg or milk to glaze

Roll out the pastry to a 35-cm/14-in square and cut this into four 18-cm/7-in squares.

To prepare the filling, melt the butter in a frying pan, add the onion and mushrooms and sauté gently until soft but not browned. Mix the sweet corn, tuna and onion mixture together and divide the mixture between the squares. Dampen the edges of each square with water and join the four corners above the middle of the filling to form an envelope. Seal and pinch the edges together then brush with beaten egg or milk. Place on a dampened baking tray and cook in a moderately hot oven (200 C, 400 F, gas 6) for 20–30 minutes. MAKES 4

Variations

Diced cooked ham or corned beef can be substituted for the tuna fish in the above recipe. If sweet corn is not one of the family's favourite foods, then try substituting defrosted frozen peas or mixed vegetables. A particularly tasty and economical combination is lightly cooked chopped bacon, grated cheese and mixed vegetables. You will need only a small quantity of bacon to give a good flavour to the filling. Any leftover cooked vegetables can be used up in this recipe.

Quick Cheese Bake

(Illustrated on page 53)

This is good and filling food for hungry children home for a hot winter tea; baked beans would go well with it.

1 kg/2 lb potatoes · salt and pepper · knob of butter
a little milk · bunch of spring onions, chopped
225 g/8 oz Cheddar cheese, grated · 1 egg, beaten

Cook the potatoes in boiling salted water until tender – about 20 minutes or 10–15 minutes if they are cut into smallish chunks. Drain them when they are cooked and mash them with a knob of butter and a little milk. Beat in the onions and cheese but reserve a little cheese for the top of the bake. Add the egg and mix well.

Grease an ovenproof dish, then turn the mixture into it and press it down. Fork up the top so that it's nice and rough (it will then become crisp when cooked) and sprinkle the cheese over.

Bake in a moderately hot oven (200 C, 400 F, gas 6) for about 45 minutes. The cooked bake will be golden brown and delicious. Leave to stand for a few minutes because the potatoes will be very hot. SERVES 4–6

Note: This is a recipe which can be heated up very well for a few minutes in the microwave oven, then shot under the grill to brown the top. If you really are in a hurry, then this is also a good way of completely transforming instant mashed potatoes.

————— FREEZER TO MICROWAVE —————

Prepare the cheese and potato mixture in individual dishes which are suitable for use in both freezer and microwave. Cover with freezer film or wrap and label. From frozen, on full power in the microwave oven, one bake will be hot in 6 minutes.

On the label
Quick Cheese Bake/Date
Unwrap
Microwave: 6 minutes on full power

Chocolate Chip Loaf

(Illustrated on page 54)

225 g/8 oz self-raising flour
100 g/4 oz butter or margarine · 75 g/3 oz blanched almonds
150 g/5 oz caster sugar · 100 g/4 oz chocolate cooking dots
2 eggs, 1 separated · about 5 tablespoons milk

Grease a 1-kg/2-lb loaf tin. Place the flour in a mixing bowl, add the butter or margarine and rub between the fingers until the mixture resembles fine breadcrumbs. Cut 50 g/2 oz of the almonds into strips. Add the sugar, almonds, 75 g/3 oz of the chocolate dots, 1 egg and 1 egg yolk and enough milk to give a sticky consistency. Put the mixture into the loaf tin and brush the top with egg white. Shred the remaining almonds and place on top, brushing again with egg white. Bake in a moderately hot oven (190 C, 375 F, gas 5) for 1–1¼ hours. Remove from the oven, and top with the remaining chocolate dots while still warm.
SERVES 12

Date and Walnut Teabread

275 g/10 oz wholewheat flour · ½ teaspoon mixed spice
1 tablespoon baking powder · 100 g/4 oz stoned dates, chopped
100 g/4 oz walnuts, chopped · 75 g/3 oz clear honey
300 ml/½ pint cold strong tea · 2 eggs, lightly beaten

Grease a 1-kg/2-lb loaf tin and line the bottom with greaseproof paper. Mix the flour with the spice, baking powder, dates and walnuts. Make a well in the centre and pour in the honey, tea and eggs. Gradually work the liquid into the dry ingredients, and when thoroughly mixed, transfer to the prepared tin. Bake in a moderate oven (180 C, 350 F, gas 4) for about 1 hour 10 minutes. Test by inserting a metal skewer; if cooked the skewer will come out clean. Cool on a wire rack and serve sliced and buttered.
SERVES 12

Family Fruit Cake

(Illustrated opposite)

100 g/4 oz self-raising flour
100 g/4 oz plain wholemeal flour
pinch of nutmeg
$\frac{1}{2}$ teaspoon bicarbonate of soda
75 g/3 oz butter or margarine
100 g/4 oz caster sugar
50 g/2 oz raisins
25 g/1 oz glacé cherries
25 g/1 oz sultanas
25 g/1 oz chopped mixed peel
grated rind of 1 lemon
1 egg, beaten
6 tablespoons milk

Grease a 450-g/1-lb loaf tin and line it with greased greaseproof paper. Place the flours, nutmeg and bicarbonate of soda in a mixing bowl and rub in the butter or margarine with the fingers until the mixture resembles fine breadcrumbs. Add the sugar, fruits, peel, lemon rind, egg and milk, and mix all ingredients thoroughly to a soft, dropping consistency. Place in the loaf tin and bake in a moderate oven (180 C, 350 F, gas 4) for 50–60 minutes. Turn out and cool on a wire rack. Serve sliced and spread with butter if you like. SERVES 12

From the top: Family Fruit Cake, Tuna-time Envelopes (page 49) and Quick Cheese Bake (page 50)

Brownies

50 g/2 oz plain chocolate
65 g/2½ oz margarine
100 g/4 oz caster sugar
2 eggs, beaten
½ teaspoon vanilla essence
175 g/6 oz plain flour
¼ teaspoon salt
½ teaspoon baking powder
50 g/2 oz walnuts, chopped

Grease a square tin 20×20×5 cm/8×8×2 in. Heat the chocolate and margarine gently in a large (2.25-litre/4-pint) saucepan, stirring continuously until melted. Remove from the heat and beat in the sugar, eggs and vanilla. Stir in the dry ingredients. Spoon into the prepared tin and level the surface. Bake in a moderate oven (180 C, 350 F, gas 4) for 30–35 minutes, until the brownies begin to pull away from the sides of the tin. Cool slightly before cutting into squares and removing from the tin.
MAKES 16

Variation

A fudgier version can be made as follows. Increase the vanilla to 1 teaspoon; decrease the flour to 100 g/4 oz and omit the baking powder. Spread the mixture in a slightly larger tin, either 23×23×5 cm/9×9×2 in or 30×19×5 cm/12×7½×2 in, and bake for 20–25 minutes.

From the top: Chocolate Chip Loaf (page 51) and Wiggly Bacon Pizzas (page 46) with salad

Maids of Honour

1 (212-g/7½-oz) packet frozen puff pastry, thawed
50 g/2 oz curd cheese · 40 g/1½ oz butter
1 egg · 2 teaspoons orange juice
50 g/2 oz caster sugar · 25 g/1 oz ground almonds
few drops of almond essence · little raspberry jam

Roll out the pastry and use it to line 12 patty tins. Squeeze the cheese in a cloth to dry it, place it in a bowl, add the butter and beat together. Beat the egg and the orange juice in a separate bowl, then add the sugar and beat well. Add the ground almonds and almond essence, then combine with the cheese and butter mixture and beat well. Put about ½ teaspoon of jam in each patty tin and then cover with the mixture. Bake in a hot oven (220 C, 425 F, gas 7), for 20–25 minutes. MAKES 12

Gingerbread

350 g/12 oz plain flour · 4 teaspoons ginger
3 teaspoons cinnamon · 225 g/8 oz margarine
225 g/8 oz soft brown sugar · 225 g/8 oz black treacle
2 eggs, beaten · 300 ml/½ pint milk
2 teaspoons bicarbonate of soda

Grease a 20 × 30-cm/8 × 12-in cake tin and line with greased greaseproof paper. Place the flour, ginger and cinnamon in a mixing bowl. Put the margarine, sugar and treacle in a saucepan and melt over a low heat. Then cool slightly and mix with the beaten eggs. Warm the milk to lukewarm and stir in the bicarbonate of soda. Make a well in the centre of the flour and pour in the liquid ingredients, the milk last, and beat thoroughly with a wooden spoon. When thoroughly mixed pour into the cake tin and bake in a cool oven (150 C, 300 F, gas 2) for 1½–2 hours. Leave to cool in the tin for a few minutes then turn out on a wire rack. SERVES 12–14

Biscuits and Cookies

Home-baked biscuits and cookies really do taste so much better than the packet varieties and they needn't contain nearly as much sugar. This chapter offers several recipes for savoury biscuits which are ideal for a quick snack with a piece of cheese, a stick of celery, a carrot or an apple. Surprisingly, children often prefer this sort of savoury snack to lots of sweet stuff which will gradually rot their teeth.

Some deliciously crunchy sweet biscuits are included too and they will go very well with a warm drink at bedtime or they can be included in a lunch box for a special treat. Once the cooked biscuits have cooled completely, they can be stored in an airtight biscuit tin for one to two weeks but you will probably have to hide the tin if you want to keep them that long!

Cheese Mice

(Illustrated on page 71)

175 g/6 oz plain flour · ¼ teaspoon salt
50 g/2 oz ground almonds · 100 g/4 oz butter or margarine
100 g/4 oz Gruyère cheese, finely grated
1 egg, lightly beaten, plus 1 egg yolk · 1 tablespoon water
flaked almonds · currants · thin string

Lightly grease two baking trays. Using a piece of cardboard cut a mouse shape 6 cm/2½ in long. Sift together the flour and salt, then stir in the ground almonds. Using your fingers, rub in the butter or margarine until the mixture resembles fine breadcrumbs. Stir in the cheese, then add the beaten egg and mix well to make a pliable dough.

Knead lightly then wrap the dough in cling film and chill it for 30 minutes, or longer if you have time. Roll the dough out on a lightly floured board to a thickness of 3 mm/⅛ in. Cut it into shapes using the cardboard pattern as a guide. Carefully transfer the shapes to the prepared baking trays. Beat the egg yolk with the water and lightly brush the glaze over the biscuits. Press two flaked almonds into each dough shape at an angle to represent ears and press in currants for eyes. Add a short length of string to form a tail.

Bake the cheese mice in a moderate oven (180 C, 350 F, gas 4) for about 15–20 minutes or until lightly browned. Remove the hot biscuits from the trays and cool them on a wire rack. MAKES 18

Quicky Cheese Straws

(Illustrated on page 71)

Use any scraps of short or puff pastry and roll out very thinly. Cover liberally with grated cheese and fold in half. Cut into 1 × 13-cm/½ × 5-in strips, glaze with beaten egg and sprinkle on cayenne pepper, nuts or seeds. Twist the straws. Bake in a hot oven (220 C, 425 F, gas 7) for 5–7 minutes until golden brown.

Sesame Squares

(Illustrated on page 71)

225 g/8 oz wholemeal flour
$\frac{1}{2}$ teaspoon salt
$\frac{1}{2}$ teaspoon grated nutmeg
150 g/5 oz butter or margarine
$\frac{3}{4}$ teaspoon wholegrain mustard
100 g/4 oz sesame seeds
50 g/2 oz cracked wheat
1 egg, lightly beaten

Lightly grease two baking trays. Mix the flour with the salt and nutmeg then, using your fingers, rub in the butter or margarine and the mustard until the mixture resembles fine breadcrumbs. Stir in the sesame seeds and cracked wheat and bind to a firm dough with the beaten egg.

Knead lightly and roll out on a floured board to a rectangle measuring 25 × 30 cm/10 × 12 in. Trim then cut into 5-cm/2-in squares, using a sharp knife. Transfer to the prepared baking trays and bake in a moderately hot oven (190 C, 375 F, gas 5) for about 15–20 minutes or until lightly browned. Remove the hot biscuits from the trays and cool on a wire rack. Makes 30

Twisters

175 g/6 oz plain flour
¼ teaspoon salt
½ teaspoon mustard powder
50 g/2 oz butter or margarine
100 g/4 oz Cheddar cheese, finely grated
1 egg, lightly beaten
1 tablespoon Marmite or yeast extract

Lightly grease two baking trays. Sift together the flour, salt and mustard powder then, using your fingers, rub in the butter or margarine until the mixture resembles fine breadcrumbs. Stir in the cheese and bind to a firm dough with the egg.

Knead lightly, then wrap the dough in cling film and chill for 1–2 hours. Divide the dough in half and roll each piece into a 20-cm/8-in square. Gently warm the Marmite or yeast extract in a small saucepan and brush over the surface of one square of dough then, using a rolling pin to help you, carefully lay the second sheet of dough over the first and cut it into 1-cm/½-in strips. Twist each strip loosely, place them slightly apart on the prepared baking trays and bake in a moderately hot oven (190 C, 375 F, gas 5) for 10–12 minutes, or until golden. Remove the hot biscuits from the trays and cool on a wire rack. MAKES 16

Oaties

50 g/2 oz plain flour
175 g/6 oz pinhead oatmeal
50 g/2 oz rolled oats
pinch of bicarbonate of soda
pinch of salt
100 g/4 oz butter or margarine
1 egg yolk

Lightly grease two baking trays. Mix together the flour, oatmeal, rolled oats, bicarbonate of soda and salt. Rub in the fat with your fingers until the mixture resembles fine breadcrumbs, then mix to a firm dough with the egg yolk. Knead lightly and roll out on a floured board to a thickness of 5 mm/¼ in. Cut into rounds using a 6-cm/2½-in plain cutter, and carefully transfer to the prepared baking trays. Bake the oaties in a moderate oven (180 C, 350 F, gas 4) for about 15–20 minutes or until darker in colour. Remove from the trays and cool on a wire rack. MAKES ABOUT 20

Variations

Bacon Oaties: Grill 75 g/3 oz rindless streaky bacon until crisp. Drain on absorbent kitchen paper then crumble finely. Stir into the rubbed-in mixture before binding to a dough with the egg yolk.
Cheese Oaties: Stir 75 g/3 oz finely grated mature Cheddar cheese into the rubbed-in mixture before binding to a dough with the egg yolk.
Herby Oaties (*Illustrated on page 71*)**:** Add 1 teaspoon each of dried rosemary and dried thyme to the dry ingredients before rubbing in the fat.

Barbecue Bites

(Illustrated on pages 134/135)

100 g/4 oz self-raising flour
100 g/4 oz plain flour
¼ teaspoon salt
1 teaspoon chilli powder
½ teaspoon ground cumin
100 g/4 oz butter or margarine
100 g/4 oz Gruyère cheese, finely grated
1 egg, lightly beaten, plus 1 egg yolk
1 tablespoon tomato purée
1 tablespoon water

Lightly grease two baking trays. Sift together the flours, salt, chilli powder and cumin. Rub in the butter or margarine with your fingers until the mixture resembles fine breadcrumbs. Stir in the cheese, then add the beaten egg and tomato purée and mix well to make a pliable dough.

Knead lightly, then wrap the dough in cling film and chill it for 30 minutes, or longer if you have time. Roll the dough out on a lightly floured board to a thickness of 3 mm/⅛ in. Cut it into shapes, using a selection of small cocktail cutters, and then carefully transfer the shapes to the prepared baking trays. Beat the egg yolk with the water, lightly brush the glaze over the biscuits, and bake in a moderate oven (180 C, 350 F, gas 4) for about 15 minutes, or until lightly browned. Remove the hot biscuits from the trays and cool on a wire rack. Continue cooking batches of biscuits in this way until all the mixture is used, cleaning and re-greasing the trays if necessary.
MAKES ABOUT 180

Pinwheel Savouries

1 (212-g/7½-oz) packet frozen puff pastry, thawed
2 (120-g/4½-oz) cans sardines in oil
100 g/4 oz full-fat soft cheese
1 teaspoon dried chives
grated rind and juice of 1 lemon

Grease a baking tray. Roll out the pastry to an oblong measuring
18 × 35 cm/7 × 14 in. Mash the sardines with their oil then beat in
the remaining ingredients and spread evenly over the pastry.
Roll up from the long side to give a 35-cm/14-in long roll. Chill
thoroughly. Cut the roll vertically into 36 slices then arrange them
placed well apart on the baking tray and bake in a moderately hot
oven (200 C, 400 F, gas 6) for 10–15 minutes. MAKES 36

Variation

Bacon and Onion Filling: Finely chop 1 small onion and 50 g/2 oz
lean bacon. Melt 25 g/1 oz butter in a pan and sauté the bacon and
onion until just cooked. Cool. Beat into 100 g/4 oz full-fat soft
cheese and use as above.

Nutty Numbers

(Illustrated on page 72)

100 g/4 oz butter or margarine
100 g/4 oz soft light brown sugar
1 egg, lightly beaten
350 g/12 oz plain flour
1 teaspoon mixed spice
1 teaspoon cinnamon
Decoration
1 egg white, lightly beaten
50 g/2 oz chopped mixed nuts
caster sugar to sprinkle

Lightly grease two baking trays and cut several number-shaped patterns from stiff cardboard. Cream the butter or margarine with the sugar until very soft, light and fluffy. Gradually add the whole egg, beating continuously. Sift together the flour and spices, then stir these dry ingredients into the creamed mixture to form a fairly firm dough.

Knead lightly and roll out on a floured board to a thickness of 5 mm/¼ in. Lay each cardboard number shape on top of the dough and cut around the edges with a knife. Carefully transfer the shapes to the prepared baking trays, brush lightly with the remaining beaten egg white and sprinkle with nuts. Bake in a moderate oven (180C, 350F, gas 4) for 15–20 minutes or until lightly browned. Remove the biscuits from the oven and immediately sprinkle them with a little caster sugar, then transfer them to a wire rack to cool. MAKES ABOUT 40 (depending on the size of the numbers).

Muesli Biscuits

225 g/8 oz muesli or muesli-type cereal
1 teaspoon cinnamon
100 g/4 oz margarine · 2 tablespoons honey
1 egg, beater · 25 g/1 oz plain flour

Mix the muesli and cinnamon together in a bowl. Melt the margarine and honey over a low heat, and add the muesli and cinnamon, then the beaten egg and flour, and mix well.

Pour into a greased 18-cm/7-in square shallow tin and bake in a cool oven (150C, 300F, gas 2) for 45 minutes. Cool slightly in the tin then mark into squares with a sharp knife. Leave in the tin until cold before cutting. MAKES 16

Chocolate Chip and Nut Cookies

(Illustrated on page 72)

100 g/4 oz butter or margarine, softened
100 g/4 oz demerara sugar · 1 egg, lightly beaten
$\frac{1}{2}$ teaspoon vanilla essence
50 g/2 oz walnuts, roughly chopped
175 g/6 oz self-raising flour · 50 g/2 oz chocolate chips

Lightly grease two baking trays. Cream the butter or margarine with the sugar until very soft, light and fluffy. Gradually add the egg, beating continuously, then beat in the vanilla essence. Stir the walnuts into the creamed mixture together with the flour and chocolate chips.

Drop heaped teaspoonfuls of the mixture, sufficiently apart to allow room for spreading, on to the prepared baking trays and flatten slightly with the back of a fork. Bake in a moderate oven (160C, 325F, gas 3) for 15–20 minutes, or until golden. Leave the cookies on the trays for a few minutes then cool on a wire rack. MAKES 30

Peanut Butter Cookies

(Illustrated on page 72)

75 g/3 oz butter or margarine
225 g/8 oz peanut butter
175 g/6 oz soft light brown sugar
1 egg
$\frac{1}{2}$ teaspoon vanilla essence
175 g/6 oz plain flour
1 teaspoon baking powder
$\frac{1}{4}$ teaspoon salt
30 salted peanuts

Grease two baking trays. Cream the butter or margarine with the peanut butter until smooth. Add the sugar, and cream again until light and fluffy. Beat in the egg and vanilla essence. Sift together the flour, baking powder and salt and fold the dry ingredients into the butter mixture, mixing thoroughly. Divide the dough into 30 and roll each portion into a ball. Place them at intervals on the baking trays, allowing space for the biscuits to spread. Flatten slightly with the prongs of a fork and place a peanut in the centre of each. Bake them in a moderately hot oven (190 C, 375 F, gas 5) for about 10 minutes or until firm and golden. Cool on a wire rack.
MAKES 30

Gingerbread Men

450 g/1 lb plain flour · ¼ teaspoon salt
2 teaspoons bicarbonate of soda · 2 teaspoons ginger
1 teaspoon cinnamon
100 g/4 oz butter or margarine
225 g/8 oz soft light brown sugar
4 tablespoons golden syrup
1 egg, lightly beaten
½ quantity glacé icing (page 80)

Lightly grease two baking trays and make a greaseproof paper piping bag according to the instructions (below). Sift the flour, salt, bicarbonate of soda, ginger and cinnamon into a bowl and make a well in the centre. Melt the butter or margarine, sugar and syrup in a saucepan over a low heat. Do not allow the mixture to boil. Cool slightly, then pour into the well in the dry ingredients. Add the egg and mix thoroughly to form a soft dough.

Knead the dough lightly, then roll it out on a floured board to a thickness of 5 mm/¼ in. Cut the dough into shapes, using a special cutter, or draw a gingerbread man on cardboard, cut it out and use it as a pattern. Using a palette knife, carefully transfer the gingerbread men to the prepared baking trays, spacing them a little apart to allow room for spreading. Bake the biscuits in a moderate oven (160 C, 325 F, gas 3) for 20 minutes, or until darkened and cooked. Cool on a wire rack.

While the biscuits are cooling, prepare the glacé icing according to the recipe instructions and pour it into the paper piping bag. Cut a tiny hole in the point of the bag and pipe clothes and facial features on the gingerbread men. MAKES ABOUT 20 (according to the size of the cutter).

To Make a Piping Bag

Fold a 25-cm/10-in square of greaseproof paper in half diagonally to make a triangle. Take one corner of the long side and roll it up to the point of the triangle, then do the same with the third corner so as to make a cone shape. Secure the ends of the paper with a little sticky tape, fold the corner pieces down neatly and cut off just the tip of the cone so as to insert the piping nozzle.

Spicy Treats

(Illustrated on front cover)

75 g/3 oz butter or margarine
2 tablespoons golden syrup
100 g/4 oz caster sugar
115 g/4½ oz plain flour
½ teaspoon bicarbonate of soda
1–2 teaspoons mixed spice or ginger
Decoration
150 g/5 oz icing sugar mixed with a little cold water or fruit juice to
a piping consistency
food colouring (optional)

Lightly grease two baking trays. Melt the butter with the syrup
and sugar over a low heat. Sieve the flour, bicarbonate of soda
and mixed spice or ginger together then add them to the butter
and syrup and mix together well. Leave to cool. Roll out the
dough to 3 mm/⅛ in thick and cut into shapes or numbers with
biscuit cutters. Place them on the prepared baking trays and bake
in a moderate oven (180 C, 350 F, gas 4) for 10–12 minutes until
golden brown. Remove from the oven and transfer on to a wire
rack to cool. Colour the icing if liked, and pipe on to the biscuits.
Makes 24–30

Caramel Fingers

(Illustrated on front cover)

100 g/4 oz butter or margarine
50 g/2 oz caster sugar
100 g/4 oz self-raising flour
Caramel
100 g/4 oz butter or margarine
8 tablespoons sweetened condensed milk
2 tablespoons golden syrup
100 g/4 oz caster sugar
Topping
100 g/4 oz plain or milk chocolate

Grease and line an 18×28-cm/7×11-in Swiss roll tin. Cream the butter or margarine and sugar together until light and fluffy, then fold in the flour. Press the mixture evenly into the tin using the back of a metal spoon and bake in a moderate oven (180 C, 350 F, gas 4) for about 20 minutes until light golden brown.

Place all the caramel ingredients together in a heavy-based saucepan, heat gently until the sugar has dissolved then boil for 4–5 minutes, stirring all the time. Pour the caramel evenly over the cooked base and leave to cool. Melt the chocolate in a bowl over hot water and spread it over the caramel. Leave to set before cutting into fingers. MAKES ABOUT 18

Wendy's Ginger Shortbread

100 g/4 oz butter
50 g/2 oz caster sugar
100 g/4 oz self-raising flour
1 generous teaspoon ground ginger
Topping
4 generous tablespoons icing sugar
50 g/2 oz butter
3 teaspoons golden syrup

Cream the butter and sugar together until pale and soft. Sift the flour and ginger together, then add to the butter and sugar. Mix well and press into a well-greased 23-cm/9-in round tin. Bake in a moderate oven (180 C, 350 F, gas 4) for 20 minutes.

For the topping, put all the ingredients in a saucepan and melt over a low heat, stirring all the time until well mixed. Bring to the boil and cook for 1 to 2 minutes, then pour the mixture over the shortbread while both are still hot.

Leave to cool in the tin, cutting into pieces while still warm. Store in an airtight tin.

Clockwise from top right: Quicky Cheese Straws (page 58), Sesame Squares (page 59), Cheese Mice (page 58) and Herby Oaties (page 61)

Wogga Wogga Biscuits

175 g/6 oz margarine or butter
75 g/3 oz icing sugar or caster sugar
50 g/2 oz custard powder
175 g/6 oz self-raising flour

Cream the margarine or butter and sugar together until pale and soft. Add the custard powder, then the flour and mix well to make a soft dough.

Place small balls of the mixture well apart on ungreased baking trays. Press down with a fork to flatten the biscuits and to mark lines on top. Bake in a moderate oven (160 C, 325 F, gas 3) for 15 to 20 minutes. Leave on tins to cool, then store the biscuits in an airtight tin.

Note: You can use different flavoured blancmange powders instead of custard to vary both the colour and flavour of the biscuits.

From the centre of the plate: Chocolate Chip and Nut Cookies (page 65)
Peanut Butter Cookies (page 66) and Nutty Numbers (page 64)

Chocolate Shortbread

100 g/4 oz plain flour · 25 g/1 oz cornflour
25 g/1 oz cocoa powder · 100 g/4 oz butter
50 g/2 oz caster sugar, plus extra for sprinkling

Sieve the flour, cornflour and cocoa together. Cream the butter until soft then add 50 g/2 oz caster sugar and beat until the mixture is pale and creamy. Work in the flour mixture a tablespoon at a time.

Knead the shortbread and press it into a 20-cm/8-in sandwich tin. Pinch the edges and prick the shortbread well with a fork. Cut through into 12 sections using the back of a knife, then sprinkle with a little caster sugar.

Leave to chill in the refrigerator for 15 minutes, then bake in a moderate oven (160 C, 325 F, gas 3) for 35 minutes. Leave in the tin for a few minutes then cool on a wire rack. MAKES 12

Toffee Bars

225 g/8 oz soft toffees · 50 g/2 oz butter or margarine
2 tablespoons golden syrup · 50 g/2 oz cornflakes

Grease a 15 × 23-cm/6 × 9-in shallow cake tin and line the bottom with greased greaseproof paper. Place the toffees in a bowl over a saucepan of hot water. Add the butter and syrup and heat gently, stirring occasionally, until melted. Stir in the cornflakes, then press the mixture into the prepared tin and level the surface with a warm metal spoon. Mark the mixture out into bars while it is still warm. Chill the bars in the refrigerator until set, then cut along the marking. MAKES 24

Whirlies

100 g/4 oz butter or margarine, softened
100 g/4 oz caster sugar
1 egg, lightly beaten
275 g/10 oz plain flour, sifted
grated rind of 1 orange
few drops of orange food colouring
grated rind of 1 lemon
few drops of yellow food colouring

Lightly grease two baking trays. Cream the butter or margarine with the sugar until very soft, light and fluffy. Gradually add the egg, beating continuously. Divide the creamed mixture in two.

Work half the flour, the orange rind and a few drops of orange colouring into one half of the creamed mixture and the remaining flour, the lemon rind and a few drops of yellow food colouring into the other half. Knead each piece of dough lightly and roll out on a floured board to a rectangle measuring 15 × 30 cm/6 × 12 in. Using a rolling pin to help you, carefully lay the sheet of lemon-flavoured dough over the sheet of orange dough, then roll up lengthways like a Swiss roll. Wrap the roll of dough in cling film or foil and chill it overnight in the refrigerator.

Cut the roll into 5-mm/¼-in slices and place the slices at intervals on the prepared trays. Bake in a moderately hot oven (200 C, 400 F, gas 6) for 10–12 minutes, or until darkened in colour and cooked. Remove the hot biscuits from the trays and transfer them to a wire rack to cool completely. MAKES 30

Novelty Cakes

Every mum shudders at the thought of another birthday, another party and yet more birthday cake! Birthday treats are just not complete without a birthday cake even if, at the end of the day, the children prefer to eat sausage rolls and crisps.

It is not always the task of making the cake that is most difficult but it is trying to decide just what kind of cake to make that presents the problems. You will find lots of interesting ideas in this chapter and they are all fairly easy to make. There are cakes which will delight the younger children and those that will appeal to the more sophisticated youngsters. Each recipe is clearly explained and there are lots of diagrams to help you through. These are the sorts of cakes which are a treat for busy mums as well as for birthday girls and boys.

Basic Victoria Sandwich

This recipe is used as a basis for many of the cakes in this chapter. The amounts given here are referred to as a '2-egg quantity'; double the amount is a '4-egg quantity' and so on. The icings referred to are those given on pages 80/81.

100 g/4 oz butter or margarine · 100 g/4 oz caster sugar
2 eggs · 100 g/4 oz self-raising flour
Filling and decoration
3–4 tablespoons raspberry jam · icing sugar for dusting

Grease a 20-cm/8-in sandwich tin or two 18-cm/7-in sandwich tins and line the bases. Cream the butter and sugar together until light and fluffy. Beat in the eggs one at a time, adding a little of the flour with the second egg. Fold in the remaining flour using a metal spoon. Place the mixture in the tin or tins and bake in a moderate oven (160 C, 325 F, gas 3) for 35–40 minutes for the 20-cm/8-in cake and 25–35 minutes for the 18-cm/7-in cakes. Turn out and cool on a wire rack.

To assemble the cake, split the larger cake and sandwich the cakes or two halves with the raspberry jam. Lay a doily on top of the cake and sprinkle with icing sugar. Carefully lift off the doily to leave a design on the surface of the cake.

All-in-one Victoria Sandwich

Add one teaspoon of baking powder to the basic recipe. Place all the ingredients in a mixing bowl and beat with a wooden spoon until well mixed (2–5 minutes). Bake as for Basic Victoria Sandwich.

Fruit-flavoured Cake

Replace 25 g/1 oz flour with one sachet of raspberry, strawberry or banana blancmange powder. Sandwich the cooked cakes together with plain butter icing.

Orange or Lemon Victoria Sandwich

Add the grated rind of one orange or one lemon to the fat and sugar before creaming. Sandwich the cooked cakes together with orange or lemon butter icing or lemon curd.

Coffee Victoria Sandwich

Add one tablespoon instant coffee powder to the flour. Sandwich the cakes with butter icing flavoured with 1 teaspoon instant coffee dissolved in 1 tablespoon hot water.

Chocolate Victoria Sandwich

Replace 25 g/1 oz flour with 25 g/1 oz cocoa powder. Sandwich the cooked cakes together with chocolate-flavoured butter icing, fudge icing or chocolate spread.

Mocha Victoria Sandwich

Add two tablespoons cocoa and one tablespoon instant coffee powder to the flour. Sandwich the cooked cakes together with chocolate butter icing.

Coconut Victoria Sandwich

Fold in 50 g/2 oz coconut with the flour and one to two tablespoons of milk to give a dropping consistency. Sandwich the cooked cakes together with raspberry jam or lemon curd.

Tray-baked Children's Party Cakes

The following recipes are all based on a 4-egg Victoria Sandwich mixture, and the icings are on pages 80/81.
Spoon the prepared cake mixture into a base-lined and greased 18 × 33-cm/ 7 × 13-in Swiss roll tin and bake in a moderate oven (180 C, 350 F, gas 4) for 30–35 minutes.

Chocolate Mint Marbles

Divide the cake mixture into three. Blend one tablespoon of cocoa with two teaspoons hot water and stir into one portion of the mixture. Flavour the second portion with peppermint flavouring, and colour it with green colouring, and leave the remaining portion plain. Spoon the mixtures into the prepared tin, swirling through once with a knife to give a marbled effect. Bake as above and cool on a wire rack. Cover the top with fudge icing coloured green and peppermint-flavoured. Cut into 18 fingers.

Hazelnut and Caramel Cake

Add 50 g/2 oz chopped toasted hazelnuts to the cake mixture with the flour. Bake as above and cool on a wire rack. Cover the top with one quantity fudge icing made with soft brown sugar instead of icing sugar.

Traffic Lights

Make up a plain or fruit-flavoured cake mixture according to the recipes on page 77. Bake as above and cool on a wire rack. Cover the top with one quantity vanilla-flavoured butter icing and cut into 18 fingers. Decorate each finger with a row of red, orange and green fruit gums.

Snakes and Ladders

Make up a plain-flavoured Victoria Sandwich mixture, bake as above and cool on a wire rack. Cover the top with one quantity vanilla-flavoured butter icing and cut into 18 fingers. Decorate half the fingers with fruit gum snakes (buy these from a sweet shop) and the remaining half with ladders constructed from chocolate Matchmakers cut to size.

Dominoes

Make up a chocolate-flavoured cake mixture according to the recipe for Chocolate Victoria Sandwich, bake as above and cool on a wire rack. Cover the top with one quantity chocolate-flavoured butter icing and cut into 18 fingers. Fit a paper piping bag (see page 67) with a No. 2 writing nozzle and fill with a half quantity of glacé icing. Pipe a line across the middle of each finger then pipe in a number of dots from one to six at each end.

Dice

Make up an orange-flavoured cake mixture according to the recipe for Orange or Lemon Victoria Sandwich, bake as above and cool on a wire rack. Cut into 24 squares then cover the top and sides with one and a half quantities of orange-flavoured butter icing, stick one to six chocolate chips on each iced side.

Glacé Icing

225 g/8 oz icing sugar, sieved · 2–3 tablespoons water

Place the icing sugar in a basin or mixing bowl and beat in the water (use a wooden spoon) until smooth.

Orange, Lemon or Lime Glacé Icing

Replace the water with fresh fruit juice, or fruit squash.

Basic Butter Icing

75 g/3 oz butter or margarine, softened
225 g/8 oz icing sugar, sifted · about 2 tablespoons milk

Cream the butter and icing sugar in a bowl until very soft and pale. Add a little milk to give a soft icing.

Vanilla Butter Icing

Add a few drops of vanilla essence to the icing mixture.

Orange or Lemon Butter Icing

Substitute a little grated orange or lemon rind and juice for the milk.

Chocolate Butter Icing

Instead of milk, use a tablespoon cocoa powder blended with two tablespoons hot water.

Basic Fudge Icing

50 g/2 oz butter or margarine · 3 tablespoons milk
225 g/8 oz icing sugar, sieved

Place all the ingredients in a basin. Stand this over a saucepan of hot water (not boiling) and stir until melted, smooth and glossy.

Remove the pan from the heat and set the bowl aside to cool. Beat well until the mixture is thick enough to spread.

Chocolate Fudge Icing

Use only one tablespoon milk and two tablespoons hot water blended with one tablespoon cocoa powder.

Quick Fondant Icing

350 g/12 oz icing sugar, sieved · 1 egg white
1 tablespoon liquid glucose, warmed

Place all the ingredients in a mixing bowl and mix together using a palette knife. The mixture will bind together like pastry. Knead to a dough, then turn out on to a board well dredged with icing sugar and knead again until smooth and easy to handle.

To use the icing, roll out the dough approximately 5 cm/2 in larger than the surface of the cake. Brush the cake with a little egg white. Lift on the icing, then smooth it down quickly using fingertips dipped in cornflour. Ease the icing down the sides of the cake to cover it smoothly and completely. Trim off any excess and allow to harden. Do not store in an airtight tin.

American Frosting

1 egg white · 175 g/6 oz icing sugar
3 tablespoons water · 1 teaspoon lemon juice

Place all the ingredients in a basin over a saucepan of hot water. Use an electric beater to whisk the ingredients until the icing stands in peaks.

Remove the bowl from the heat and continue whisking until the icing has cooled completely. Spread the frosting over the cake. This frosting must be used as soon as it is made.

Train Cake

4-egg quantity Victoria Sandwich cake mixture (page 77) *or*
1 shop-bought loaf cake
1 Swiss Roll (page 103)
3 quantities chocolate butter icing (page 80)
a little raspberry jam (optional)
7 individual chocolate-covered Swiss rolls (shop-bought)
Smarties and Liquorice Allsorts to decorate the train
mixed sweets to fill the trucks
2 (25-cm/10-in) square cake boards, placed together

Make up the Victoria Sandwich cake following the recipe instructions. Line and grease a 1-kg/2-lb loaf tin and turn the mixture into it. Bake the cake in a moderate oven (180 C, 350 F, gas 4) for $1\frac{1}{4}$ – $1\frac{1}{2}$ hours, or until it is cooked through. Turn the cake out on to a wire rack and allow it to cool completely. Alternatively you can buy a loaf cake to make the carriages. Make up the Swiss roll following the recipe instructions, then roll it up and leave it on a wire rack to cool. (Again you can use a shop-bought cake if you would prefer not to make one.)

To assemble the train, trim the ends off the loaf cake. Make the trimmings fairly thick as they will be used to form the cab on the train. Trim the slightly uneven top off the cake. Follow the diagrams to assemble and decorate the cake. Cut all the trimmings into small oblong pieces. Sandwich them together with a smear of butter icing or jam to make an oblong shape which will sit at one end of the Swiss roll to represent a cab. Spread a little butter icing on one end of the stacked cake and put the 'cab' on top of one end of the Swiss roll. Spread a little butter icing between the cab and the curve of the roll to fill in the gaps. Cut the trimmed loaf cake vertically in half to make two small trucks.

You should now have the basic shape of the train and the trucks. Cover the pieces of cake lightly all over with a little chocolate butter icing. Rest the cakes, in line like a train, on the miniature Swiss rolls on a cake board. Allow two Swiss rolls for each piece of cake. Cut the one remaining Swiss roll in half and stand the pieces on top of the front of the cake to make a double funnel.

To add colour and to decorate the cake, press the Smarties and

Liquorice Allsorts in a circle on the very front of the train. Add a few to the cab end, then make a neat line of colourful sweets down the length of the trucks. To finish the cake pile sweets on top of the trucks. If you have any toy figures and features from a train set, then arrange them around the cake on the board, adding miniature trees and station buildings if you like.

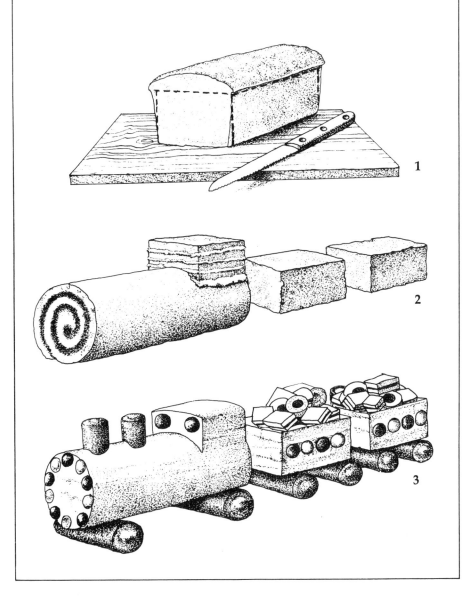

Roller Skate Cake

8-egg quantity Victoria Sandwich cake mixture (page 77)
2 quantities butter icing (page 80)
2 individual chocolate-covered Swiss rolls (shop-bought)
food colouring of your choice
2 black liquorice bootlaces
Liquorice Allsorts for decoration
25-cm/10-in square cake board

Make up the cake mixture according to the recipe instructions. Line and grease two 18×33-cm/7×13-in Swiss roll tins, then divide the mixture equally between them. Bake the cakes in a moderate oven (180C, 350F, gas 4) for 30–35 minutes. When cooked, the cakes should be risen and golden. Turn the cakes out on to a wire rack to cool.

Make up the butter icing while they are cooling. Cut a piece of greaseproof paper to the same size as the Swiss roll tin in which the cake was cooked. Draw the outline of a roller skate boot on the paper. When the cakes have cooled completely, cut out a roller boot from each one using the pattern as a guide to make them both the same size.

Use a little of the butter icing to sandwich the boot shapes together. Place the individual Swiss rolls on the cake board, then rest the boot cake on top. Colour the butter icing in the colour which you would like the roller skate to be – red or blue are both suitable. Cover the cake thinly all over with the icing. Put a dab of icing in the middle of each of the wheel ends (the Swiss rolls), then stick a Liquorice Allsort on each of them.

Press a double row of liquorice sweets down the front of the boot and stick lengths of the liquorice bootlace criss-cross style between them to represent the fastening. If you like you can add a row of sweets round the bottom of the boot. Add a bow of liquorice bootlace at the top of the fastening to complete the cake.

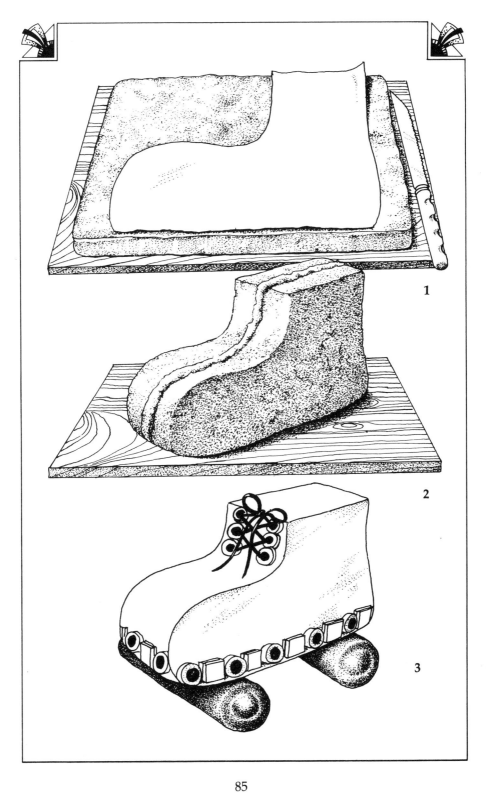

1

2

3

85

Cricket Bat Cake

4-egg quantity Victoria Sandwich cake mixture (page 77)
2 quantities butter icing (page 80)
red food colouring
1 black liquorice bootlace
30-cm/12-in square cake board

Grease and line an 18 × 33-cm/7 × 13-in Swiss roll tin. Put all but 4 tablespoons of the prepared sandwich cake mixture into the tin. Spread the mixture out evenly. Grease two patty tins and put the remaining mixture in them. Bake the large cake in a moderate oven (180C, 350F, gas 4) for 25–30 minutes, then turn it out to cool on a wire rack. Place the two small cakes in the oven and cook them for 10–15 minutes. Remove the small cakes from the tins and cool them on a wire rack.

While the cakes are cooling prepare the butter icing following the recipe instructions. Cut out a piece of greaseproof paper the same size as the Swiss roll tin used for cooking the cake, then draw the shape of a cricket bat on it.

Using the drawing of a cricket bat as a guide, cut out the shape from the cake. Trim the tops off the small cakes, then sandwich them together with a little of the butter icing. Trim away the edges of the cake as necessary to make a cricket ball.

Cover the bat shape with white butter icing, spreading it with a palette knife or round-bladed knife. Do not try to achieve a perfectly smooth surface, rather make neat lines in the butter icing.

Colour any remaining icing a good strong red and spread this all over the cricket ball (the shape made from the two small cakes). Put the ball on the cake board next to the bat. Cut the liquorice into lengths which will fit over the handle end of the bat to represent the binding, then put them neatly in place.

Use the last of the red butter icing to pipe 'Happy Birthday' and the name of the person on the bat. You can add a bow of red ribbon to the handle end of the bat if you like.

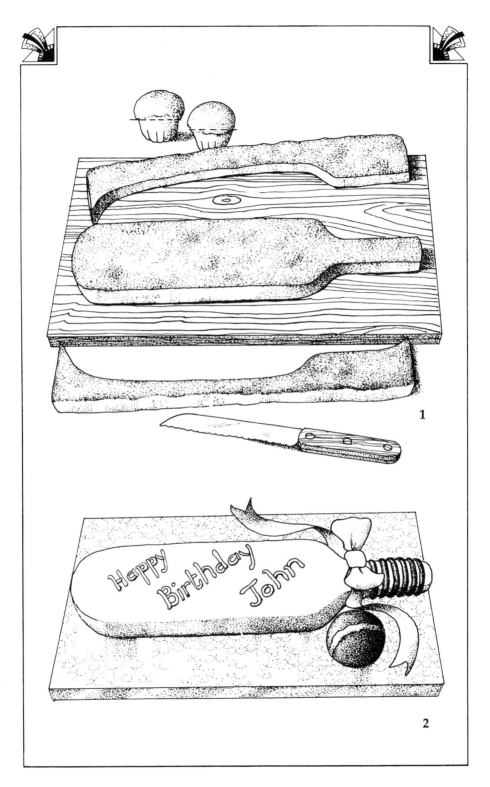

1

Happy Birthday John

2

Pencil Box Cake

2-egg quantity Victorian Sandwich cake mixture (page 77)
$\frac{1}{2}$ quantity quick fondant icing (page 81)
food colouring of your choice
100 g/4 oz apricot jam, sieved
$\frac{1}{2}$ quantity Chocolate Butter Icing (page 80)
brand new pencils, pretty and unusual rubbers, unusual pencil
sharpeners and some sweets to decorate
25-cm/10-in square cake board

Base line and grease an 11×25-cm/$4\frac{1}{2} \times 10$-in loaf tin. Make the cake mixture according to the recipe instructions, then put it into the tin and smooth the top. Bake the cake in a moderate oven (180 C, 350 F, gas 4) for 45–50 minutes until well risen and golden brown. Turn the cooked cake out to cool on a wire rack.

Meanwhile, prepare the fondant icing. If you like you can buy ready made fondant icing from cake decorating shops. Take the cooled cake and slice a thick piece off the top to make the lid of the pencil box. Use a small pointed knife to cut about 1 cm/$\frac{1}{2}$ in down into the cake, working all the way round the top 1 cm/$\frac{1}{2}$ in. in from the edge. Scoop out the cake from the middle to make a shallow box. Knead the food colouring of your choice into the icing. Take three-quarters of the icing and roll it out to cover the main piece of cake. Brush the cake with a little jam and lift the icing over it, moulding it neatly in place. Cover the small piece of cake in the same way.

Use the chocolate butter icing to pipe the words 'Pencil Box' on the top of the smaller piece of cake. Put the main cake on the board. Line the box with a piece of greaseproof paper or a cut-out doily. Arrange the pencils, rubbers, sharpeners and sweets in the box. Put the pencil box lid at an angle on top of the cake so that all the goodies from inside are showing clearly. Add extra bits and pieces to the cake board so that there are enough gifts to go round all the children. You could add some small notepads to the edge of the board if you like.

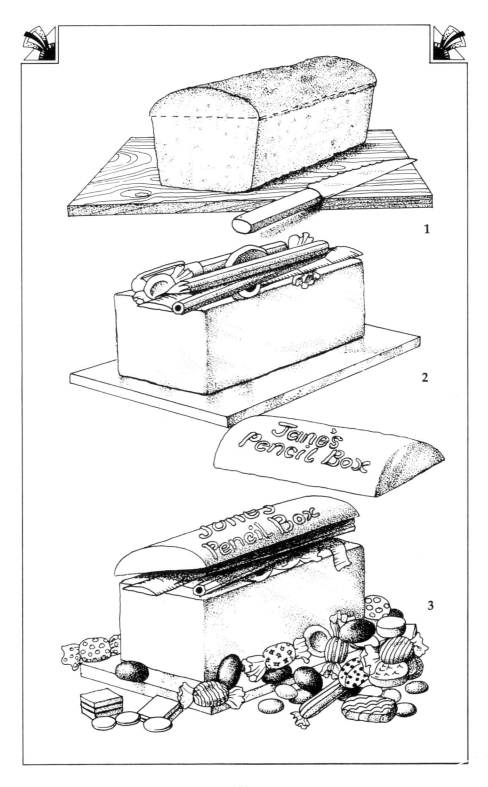

1

2

3

Clown Cake

(Illustrated on pages 134/135)

8-egg quantity Victoria Sandwich Cake mixture (page 77)
225 g/8 oz raspberry jam
double quantity Butter Icing (page 80)
pink food colour · sugar strands
Smarties · liquorice sweets
small piece of marzipan, coloured red
dolly mixtures
a large tray or board

Make up the cake mixture following the recipe instructions. Line and grease two 18 × 33-cm/7 × 13-in Swiss roll tins, then put the mixture in them and spread it out evenly. Bake the cakes in a moderate oven (180 C, 350 F, gas 5) for 25–30 minutes. Turn the cooked cakes out on to a wire rack to cool and remove the greaseproof paper. Sandwich the cooled cakes together with jam.

Take a piece of greaseproof paper and cut it to the same size as the cake. Using the diagram as a guide, draw the shape of the clown face and hat on the paper, using as much space as possible to make the cake as big as you can. Cut out the pieces of paper, then use them as a guide to cut out the shapes from the cake.

Colour the butter icing pale pink, then cover the face, hat and bow tie of the clown all over – make the layer quite thin or it will be too sickly. Put the round clown face on the board or tray. Sprinkle the sugar strands all over the hat and put it on the board or tray, pressing it against the face. Add the bow tie. Put a line of Smarties between the hat and face of the clown. Use liquorice sweets to make eyes and add the marzipan for the nose. Add liquorice sweets for the mouth and round the bow tie; lastly , from the scraps of cake which remain, cut a circle to make a bobble to go on top of the hat. Cover this with a little butter icing and put lots of dolly mixtures on it, then put it in place at the top of the hat.

The clown cake is a cheerful choice for young children; you can add birthday candles all the way up the front of the hat if you like.

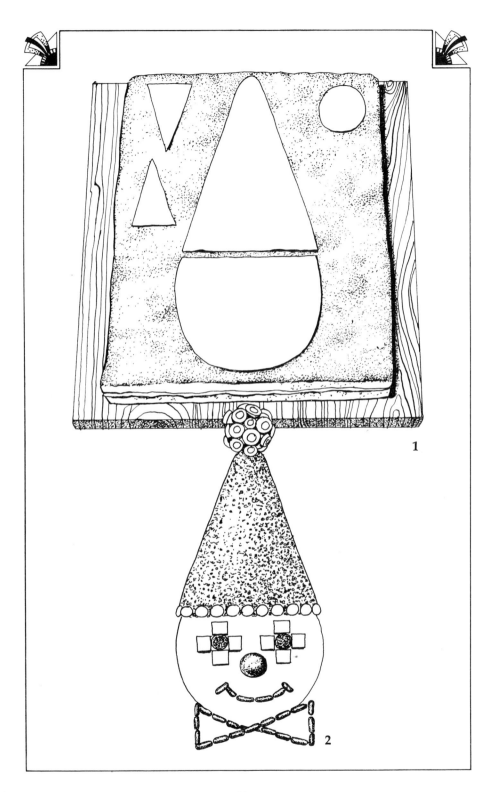

1

2

Pony Cake

8-egg quantity Victoria Sandwich Cake mixture (page 77)
100 g/4 oz raspberry jam, sieved
double quantity Butter Icing (page 80)
pink and blue food colour
1 chocolate button
pink baby ribbon
a large tray or board

Make up the cake mixture following the recipe instructions. Line and grease two 18 × 35-cm/7 × 13-in Swiss roll tins, then put the mixture in them and spread it out evenly. Bake the cakes in a moderate oven (180 C, 350 F, gas 5) for 25–30 minutes. Turn the cooked cakes out on to wire racks to cool and remove the greaseproof paper. Sandwich the cooled cakes together with jam.

Take a piece of greaseproof paper and cut it to the same size as the cake. Using the diagram as a guide, draw the shape of a pony on the paper. Cut this out and use it as a guide for cutting the cake.

Colour two-thirds of the butter icing blue and the remainder pink. Put the cake on the tray or board and cover it all over with blue icing. Put the pink icing in an icing bag fitted with a small star nozzle. Pipe pink icing along the neck to represent a mane and pipe long swirls at the back of the pony to represent a tail.

Halve the chocolate button and use one piece to represent an eye. Use the second piece to make a mouth. Decorate the cake with short lengths of ribbon to make reins and add bows of ribbon to complete the decoration.

1

2

Gingerbread House

double quantity Gingerbread Men mixture (page 67)
double quantity Royal Icing (page 115)
small pieces of red tissue paper
25-cm/10-in square cake board
sweets to decorate

Make the gingerbread mixture according to the recipe instructions. Divide the mixture in half and roll it out on a lightly floured surface. Cut out shapes to make the house following the diagrams and roughly following the dimensions.

Lay the pieces of gingerbread on greased baking trays, cut out holes for the windows and bake in a cool oven (150 C, 300 F, gas 2) for 1½ to 2 hours. Leave to cool on the trays for a few minutes, then transfer the pieces of gingerbread to a wire rack to cool completely.

Make the icing. Cut small squares of red tissue to go in the windows. Use a dab of icing to stick the tissue paper behind the windows. Use more icing to join the pieces of gingerbread together as you assemble them. Do this by spreading a little icing over the edges of the biscuit, then press the next piece firmly against it. Assemble the gingerbread house on the cake board.

Reserve some of the remaining icing to pipe the door and windows on the house, then spread the rest over the roof, teasing it down over the edge with the point of a knife so that it resembles icicles. Pipe the window frames and door on the house, then leave it until the icing has set.

Add colourful sweets to decorate the house and to represent pebbles or flowers in the garden. Put a liquorice sweet on the roof of the house to represent a chimney pot.

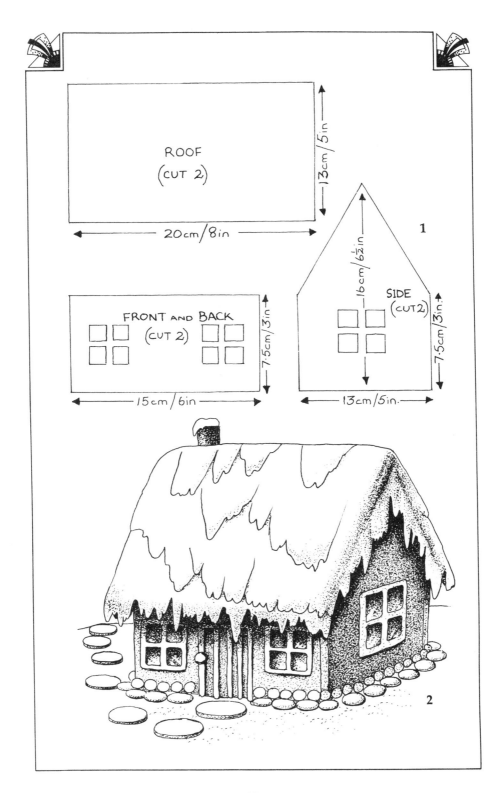

ROOF
(CUT 2)

13cm/5in

20cm/8in

1

16cm/6½in

SIDE
(CUT2)

13cm/3in.

13cm/5in.

FRONT and BACK
(CUT 2)

7.5cm/3in

15cm/6in

7.5cm/3in.

2

95

Sparkling Bonfire Cake

This cake is an excellent treat for children who celebrate their birthdays on or near the 5th of November.

2-egg quantity Victoria Sandwich cake mixture (page 77)
1 quantity Chocolate Fudge Icing (page 81)
1 box flavoured chocolate sticks (*Matchmakers*)
1 packet indoor sparklers
small piece of marzipan, moulded into a Guy Fawkes shape
20-cm/8-in round cake board

Make the cake mixture according to the recipe instructions. Thoroughly grease a 900-ml/1½-pint ovenproof pudding basin and put the mixture in it, smoothing down the top. Stand the basin on a baking tray (this makes it easier to handle), then bake the cake in a moderate oven (160 C, 325 F, gas 3) for 1 hour. Turn the cooked cake out on to a wire rack to cool.

Place the cake on the cake board and cover it all over with the fudge icing, then pile the chocolate sticks all over it to resemble logs. Stick the sparklers in the cake, pointing them outwards, so that they do not drop any ash on the icing as they burn. Lastly put the marzipan Guy Fawkes on top of the cake. Hide the cake away until the children are ready to eat it, then light the sparklers and carry it out while they are burning.

Ballet Cake

1 Victoria Sandwich cake (see page 77)
1 quantity Butter Icing (page 80)
pink food colour
100 g/4 oz raspberry jam
1 quantity Glaće Icing (page 80)
1 packet Iced Gems (the small biscuits with a
swirl of icing on top)
ballerina doll (available from cake decorating
shops or most stores which sell cake decorations)
a few tiny flowers, fresh or made from fabric
25-cm/10-in round cake board

Make the Victoria Sandwich according to the recipe instructions. Colour the butter icing pale pink. Sandwich the cake together with the jam, then place it on the board. Use about two-thirds of the butter icing to cover the sides of the cake, spreading it evenly but thinly.

Put a small star nozzle in a piping bag, then put the remaining butter icing in the bag. Pipe a row of stars all round the edge of the cake. Make the glaće icing and leave it white, then pour it gently on top of the cake, spreading it very lightly so that it floods the top completely and thinly. Leave this to set.

To decorate the cake, put the ballerina doll in the middle. Put the Iced Gems at intervals in the piped stars round the edge of the cake, then dot a few flowers over the top of the cake. The tiny rosebuds which can be bought to decorate wedding cakes are ideal for the top of the cake. The Iced Gems represent the footlights and the flowers have been thrown on to the stage (the top of the cake) by the audience.

Butterfly Cake

(Illustrated on front cover)

175 g/6 oz butter or margarine, at room temperature
175 g/6 oz caster sugar
3 eggs, beaten
175 g/6 oz self-raising flour, sieved
4–6 tablespoons raspberry jam
Icing and Decoration
175 g/6 oz butter or margarine
350 g/12 oz icing sugar, sieved
pink food colouring
1 chocolate flake
pink or red dragees, fruit polos and sugared diamond jellies
cake candles
25-cm/10-in square cake board

Grease two 18–20-cm/7–8-in sandwich tins. Cream the butter or margarine and sugar together until light and fluffy. Gradually beat in the eggs a little at a time, beating well between each addition. Fold in the flour and mix to a smooth consistency. Divide the mixture between the two tins, and bake for 25–30 minutes in a moderately hot oven (190 C, 375 F, gas 5) until light golden brown. Turn out and cool on a wire rack.

Sandwich the cakes together with raspberry jam and then cut in half. Place the two halves back to back (*Diagram 1*) and cut a triangular wedge (*Diagram 2*) to make the wings. Cream the butter and sugar together until soft and smooth and colour with a few drops of the pink food colouring. Cover the top and sides of the cake with the cream using a round-bladed knife. Use the chocolate flake for the butterfly's body and decorate it with the sweets to make pretty patterns. Lastly add birthday cake candles. Use any left-over cake for trifles.

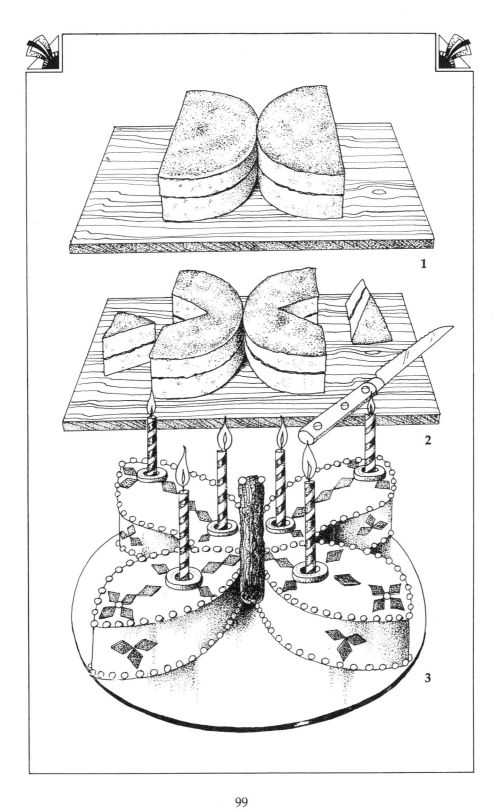

1

2

3

Pram Christening Cake

8-egg quantity Victoria Sandwich Cake mixture (page 77)
100 g/4 oz raspberry jam, sieved
double quantity Butter Icing (page 80)
pink or blue food colouring
tiny sugared flowers in pink or blue (to contrast
with the butter icing)
silver dragees · 25-cm/10-in square cake board

Make up the cake mixture following the recipe instructions. Line and grease two 18 × 35-cm/7 × 13-in Swiss roll tins, then divide the mixture between them and spread it out evenly. Bake the cakes in a moderate oven (180 C, 350 F, gas 5) for 25 to 35 minutes, then turn them out to cool on a wire rack and remove the greaseproof paper.

Cut out a piece of greaseproof paper to the same size as the cakes. Following the diagrams as a guide, draw the shape of a pram on the paper using the whole of the area to make the pattern as large as possible. Using this paper pattern as a guide, cut out the pram shape from each of the cakes, then sandwich both pieces together with the jam. Place the cake on the board.

To decorate the cake, spread a little butter icing evenly all over it, making neat marks with the knife. Colour the remaining butter icing either pink or blue. Put a small plain piping nozzle in a piping bag and fill it with the butter icing. Pipe the shape of the wheels of the parm and pipe the name of the baby on the side. Place the tiny sugared flowers in a line down the edge of the hood and add silver dragees in between the flowers. Place a small flower in the middle of each wheel to complete the decoration.

Note: this is a very simple christening cake; if you prefer you can cover the cake shape in fondant icing (either shop bought or home made, see page 81), moulding it carefully over the edges of the sponge cake. The name of the child and the decoration can then be piped on to the cake in pink or blue royal icing (see page 115) or in butter icing if you find this easier. Using the above recipe is easier and ideal if you do not want to spend many hours fiddling around with the icing.

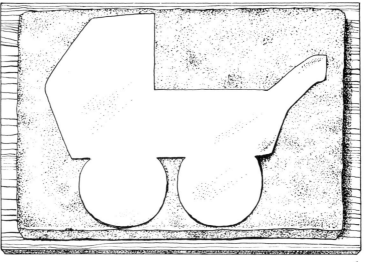

1

2

Weekend Cakes

Weekends are family times when everyone is at home and friends come to visit. In most homes this means chaos – people dashing about doing their favourite sport, digging the garden (and bringing lots of it in on their shoes) or spending time on a new hobby.

Somewhere in the middle of all the activity, poor old mum tries to retain her sanity and make sure that there is plenty of food for all the meals, for the visitors and for those in-between-meal snacks. This is also the time when everyone thinks that a cake would be rather nice for tea; on these occasions you need a recipe that works well without spending hours in the kitchen. You will find lots of ideas here for cakes which are quite special enough for Sunday tea without being complicated enough to require a whole day's cooking on Saturday.

Swiss Roll

(Illustrated on page 106)

50 g/2 oz caster sugar, plus a little for sprinkling
2 eggs, beaten · 50 g/2 oz plain flour
225 g/8 oz raspberry jam

Grease and base line an 18 × 28-cm/7 × 11-in Swiss roll tin. Place the sugar and eggs in a mixing bowl over a saucepan of hot water and whisk until the mixture is thick and pale in colour and forms a trail when lifted. Sieve the flour twice and fold into the mixture. Place the mixture in the Swiss roll tin, smoothing over evenly, and bake in a moderately hot oven (200 C, 400 F, gas 6) for 8–10 minutes.

Meanwhile, place a damp tea-towel on a working surface and lay a sheet of greaseproof paper on top. Sprinkle very lightly with caster sugar. As soon as the Swiss roll is cooked turn it out on to the sugared paper. Remove the lining paper and trim the crusty edges. Cut lightly but not right through the cake along the shortest edge nearest to you; this will ensure that the cake rolls up neatly. Spread the jam evenly over the Swiss roll, then roll it up tightly. Leave the tea-towel around the roll for about 30 seconds, then allow to cool on a wire rack.

Chocolate Swiss Roll

Replace 15 g/½ oz flour with 15 g/½ oz cocoa powder. Roll a piece of greaseproof paper in the cake instead of the jam, then allow to cool. Carefully unroll the cooled cake and fill it with chocolate nut spread. Roll up again and sift a little icing sugar over the roll before serving.

Fruit Surprise Cake

(Illustrated opposite)

2 quantities Swiss Roll mixture (page 103)
1 (425-g/15-oz) can fruit, e.g. black cherries, sliced peaches,
mandarin oranges etc.
1 packet Quick Jel
300 ml/½ pint double cream
a little sieved icing sugar

Grease and base line two 20-cm/8-in Victoria sandwich tins. Prepare the cake mixture according to the recipe instructions and spoon into the prepared tins. Bake in a moderately hot oven (190 C, 375 F, gas 5) for 20–25 minutes or until well risen and firm to the touch. Leave in the tins for a few minutes then leave to cool on a wire rack.

Now fill the cake. Drain the fruit, reserving the juice and a few pieces of fruit, and arrange it on one sponge. Use the reserved fruit juice to make up the Quick Jel according to the packet instructions, leave until half set then pour over the fruit and leave to set. When set whisk the cream until thick enough to hold its shape and use half to sandwich the cake layers together. Dredge the top of the cake with icing sugar. Fill a piping bag fitted with a large star nozzle with the remaining cream and pipe swirls of cream around the edge of the cake. Decorate with the reserved fruit.

Fruit Surprise Cake and a slice of Refrigerator Cake (page 112)

Cherry Buns

(Illustrated opposite)

175 g/6 oz self-raising flour
75 g/3 oz butter or margarine
100 g/4 oz sugar
50 g/2 oz desiccated coconut
75 g/3 oz glacé cherries, halved
1 egg plus 1 egg yolk
milk if necessary
Decoration
1 egg white
25 g/1 oz desiccated coconut
6–8 glacé cherries, halved

Grease two baking trays. Sieve the flour, rub in the butter or margarine with your fingers until the mixture resembles fine breadcrumbs then add the sugar, coconut, halved cherries, the egg and egg yolk. If the eggs are large and the cherries juicy there may be enough liquid to make a sticky consistency, otherwise add just a little milk. Put the mixture in 12–16 small heaps on the trays, flattening slightly. Brush with egg white, sprinkle with coconut, and press half a glacé cherry on top of each cake. Bake for 12–15 minutes in a hot oven (230 C, 450 F, gas 8). Allow the cakes to cool for a few minutes on the baking trays, then transfer to a wire cooling rack. MAKES 12–16

Plain and Chocolate Swiss Rolls (page 103) with Cherry Buns

107

Chocolate Fudge Cake

225 g/8 oz self-raising flour
25 g/1 oz cocoa powder
100 g/4 oz soft margarine
2 eggs, lightly beaten
1 (170-g/6-oz) can evaporated milk
1 teaspoon vanilla essence
1 quantity chocolate fudge icing (page 81)

Lightly grease and base line two 20-cm/8-in sandwich tins. Sift together the flour and cocoa. Make a well in the centre and add all the remaining ingredients. Beat together with a wooden spoon or an electric mixer for 3 minutes or until the mixture is a soft dropping consistency and has become paler in colour. Divide between the prepared tins and level the surface. Bake in a moderate oven (180 C, 350 F, gas 4) for 30–35 minutes or until darker and firm to the touch. Cool in the tins for a few minutes, then turn out on a wire rack to cool completely.

Make the icing according to the recipe instructions and use a quarter of it to sandwich the cake together, spreading the rest of the icing over the top and sides with a palette knife.

Orange and Walnut Loaf

50 g/2 oz butter
175 g/6 oz caster sugar
1 egg, beaten
grated rind and juice of 1 orange
200 g/7 oz plain flour
2 teaspoons baking powder
$\frac{1}{2}$ teaspoon salt
2 tablespoons milk
50 g/2 oz walnut pieces

Grease a 1-kg/2-lb loaf tin. Cream the butter and sugar together until light and fluffy then add the egg with the grated orange rind and juice and mix well. Sift the flour with the baking powder and salt. Add the milk alternately with the sifted flour to the creamed butter mixture. Finally fold in the walnut pieces. Put into the greased loaf tin and bake in a moderately hot oven (190 C, 375 F, gas 5) for 1 hour. Turn out and leave to cool on a wire rack. Serve sliced and spread with butter.

Chocolate Boxes

4-egg quantity chocolate Victoria Sandwich cake
mixture (page 77)
350 g/12 oz plain chocolate
2 quantities chocolate butter icing (page 80)
1(298-g/10½-oz) can mandarin segments, drained
8 glacé cherries, halved

Lightly grease and base line a 20-cm/8-in square cake tin. Prepare
the cake mixture according to the recipe instructions and spoon
into the prepared tin, smoothing the surface and making a slight
hollow in the centre. Bake in a moderate oven (160 C, 325 F, gas 3)
for 1 hour or until well risen and firm to the touch. Cool in the tin
for a few minutes then turn out on to a wire rack to cool
completely.

Meanwhile, melt the chocolate in a bowl over a saucepan of hot
water. Spread a thin coat of chocolate 40 cm/16 in square over a
piece of waxed or non-stick baking parchment and leave until set.
Cut the cake into 16 (5-cm/2-in) cubes. Spread five sides of each
cake with the chocolate butter icing. Cut the chocolate into 5-cm/
2-in squares, press these on to the four sides of each cake, and
decorate the tops with four mandarin segments each and a
halved glacé cherry. MAKES 16

Note: You can use plain, shop-bought Madeira cake to make this
recipe if you like.

Iced Fancies

(Illustrated on pages 134/135)

2 quantities Swiss Roll mixture (page 103)
Icing and decoration
1 quantity glacé icing (page 80)
food colourings
1 quantity butter icing (page 80)
various small sweets, cake decorations, chocolate buttons
or vermicelli

Grease and line a 23×33-cm/9×13-in Swiss roll tin. Prepare the cake mixture according to the recipe instructions and pour into the prepared tin. Bake in a moderately hot oven (200 C, 400 F, gas 6) for 10–12 minutes or until well risen and firm to the touch. Turn out and allow to cool on a wire rack.

Cut the cake into small squares, diamonds and oblong shapes. A biscuit cutter may be used to cut out rounds of cake, but this does produce wasted cuttings.

The glacé icing can be any colour you choose, but the shades should be delicate. Divide it into several portions and add a few drops of food colouring to each. Cover the cake shapes in glacé icing and leave to set slightly. Colour the butter icing in similar delicate shades, place it in a piping bag fitted with a small star nozzle and pipe decorations on the cakes. Finish decorating with various sweets, or alternatively the sides of the cakes can be spread with butter icing and coated in grated chocolate, chopped nuts, coconut or sugar strands. The top of the cakes should be iced with glacé icing and decorated with piped butter icing.
Makes about 30

Refrigerator Cake

(Illustrated on page 105)

225 g/8 oz butter
2 eggs, beaten
25 g/1 oz caster sugar
225 g/8 oz plain chocolate
225 g/8 oz digestive, chocolate or gingernut biscuits
Decoration
150ml/¼ pint double cream, whipped
glacé cherries
angelica

Grease a 15-cm/6-in loose-bottomed cake tin. Melt the butter in a bowl over a pan of boiling water. Meanwhile, beat the eggs with the sugar in another bowl and when thoroughly combined, pour the melted butter into the mixture, beating continuously. Melt the chocolate in a bowl over boiling water and add this to the butter mixture.

Break up the biscuits into small pieces and fold into the chocolate mixture. Turn the mixture into the cake tin, smoothing the top with a palette knife. Chill overnight in the refrigerator.

Push the cake out of the tin by loosening the base and turn on to a serving dish. Decorate with swirls of whipped cream, glacé cherries and pieces of angelica. SERVES 6–8

Cheesecake

225 g/8 oz Sweet Flan Pastry (page 10)
25 g/1 oz cornflour
100 g/4 oz caster sugar
450 ml/¾ pint milk
50 g/2 oz butter
few drops of vanilla essence
grated rind of 1 lemon
225 g/8 oz full-fat soft cheese
3 eggs, separated
icing sugar to dust

Prepare the pastry according to the recipe and use to line a 25-cm/ 10-in loose-bottomed flan tin. Bake blind in a moderately hot oven (200 C, 400 F, gas 6) for 15 minutes, then remove the paper or foil and beans.

To make the filling, blend the cornflour with the sugar and a little milk until smooth. Heat the remaining milk and stir it into the cornflour, then return it to the pan and bring it to the boil. Remove the pan from the heat and stir in the butter, vanilla essence and lemon rind. Finally, beat in the soft cheese and egg yolks and allow the mixture to cool.

Whisk the egg whites until stiff and fold into the cooled mixture. Turn the cheese mixture into the flan case and bake it for a further 25–35 minutes until lightly browned and set. Cool completely. Before serving, dust the top of the cheesecake with icing sugar. SERVES 8

Seasonal Treats

All families have their own traditions for the annual holidays and most celebrations include a cake or some other baked goodies. In this chapter you will find recipes for Christmas, Easter and bonfire night. Small and large cakes, mince pies, hot cross buns and some favourite bonfire night flapjacks are all included.

These are the times when the children will want to help with the cooking and these are the recipes you will be likely to pass on to future generations. When everyone has had a go at the cooking they will all want to gather round and help to eat these seasonal delights.

Snow-topped Christmas Cake

20-cm/8-in round cake tin quantity rich fruit cake (page 116)
Almond Paste
350 g/12 oz ground almonds
175 g/6 oz caster sugar
175 g/6 oz icing sugar, sieved
3 egg whites
few drops of almond essence
3 tablespoons apricot jam, sieved
Royal Icing
4 egg whites
900 g/2 lb icing sugar, sieved
4 teaspoons lemon juice
2 teaspoons glycerine

Make the fruit cake according to the recipe instructions and leave to cool in the tin before turning out.

Mix the ground almonds and sugar in a bowl, then blend in the egg whites and almond essence to make a soft paste. Knead until smooth and then divide into three equal portions. Roll one piece on a sugared board to a 20-cm/8-in circle. Roll the remaining two-thirds to a strip the same depth as the cake and long enough to go all the way round it. Brush the sides and top of the cake with apricot jam. Place the long strip round the sides and press firmly to join. Place the circle of paste on top of the cake. Allow the almond paste to dry for at least 3 days before icing or it will discolour the icing.

Whisk the egg whites until frothy, then add the sugar, a tablespoon at a time, beating well after each addition. Finally beat in the lemon juice and glycerine. To prevent the icing hardening, cover the bowl with a damp cloth.

Spread the icing thickly over the top and round the sides of the cake and draw it up in peaks with the handle of a teaspoon. Leave for a day to set then decorate as desired.

Rich Fruit Cakes

This rich fruit cake is suitable for all types of special occasions, such as weddings, christenings, Christmas and birthday cakes.

Round	18 cm/7 in	20 cm/8 in	23 cm/9 in	25 cm/10 in
Square	15 cm/6 in	18 cm/7 in	20 cm/8 in	23 cm/9 in
Butter	100 g/4 oz	150 g/5 oz	200 g/7 oz	250 g/9 oz
Dark Soft Brown Sugar	150 g/5 oz	175 g/6 oz	225 g/8 oz	275 g/10 oz
Black Treacle	1 tablespoon	1 tablespoon	1 tablespoon	1 tablespoon
Eggs	3	4	5	6
Plain Flour	175 g/6 oz	200 g/7 oz	250 g/9 oz	300 g/11 oz
Ground Mixed Spice	$\frac{3}{4}$ teaspoon	1 teaspoon	$1\frac{1}{4}$ teaspoons	$1\frac{1}{2}$ teaspoons
Grated Nutmeg	$\frac{1}{4}$ teaspoon	$\frac{1}{2}$ teaspoon	$\frac{1}{2}$ teaspoon	$\frac{3}{4}$ teaspoon
Ground Almonds	40 g/$1\frac{1}{2}$ oz	50 g/2 oz	65 g/$2\frac{1}{2}$ oz	75 g/3 oz
Grated Rind	1 lemon	1 lemon	1 lemon	2 lemons
Grated Rind	1 orange	1 orange	1 orange	2 oranges
Chopped Almonds	50 g/2 oz	65 g/$2\frac{1}{2}$ oz	90 g/$3\frac{1}{2}$ oz	100 g/4 oz
Glacé Cherries	50 g/2 oz	65 g/$2\frac{1}{2}$ oz	90 g/$3\frac{1}{2}$ oz	100 g/4 oz
Raisins	75 g/3 oz	100 g/4 oz	150 g/5 oz	175 g/6 oz
Sultanas	150 g/5 oz	200 g/7 oz	250 g/9 oz	300 g/11 oz

Round	18 cm/7 in	20 cm/8 in	23 cm/9 in	25 cm/10 in
Square	15 cm/6 in	18 cm/7 in	20 cm/8 in	23 cm/9 in
Currants	225 g/8 oz	275 g/10 oz	375 g/13 oz	450 g/1 lb
Chopped Mixed Peel	50 g/2 oz	65 g/2½ oz	90 g/3½ oz	100 g/4 oz
Brandy	1 tablespoon	2 tablespoons	2 tablespoons	3 tablespoons
Orange Juice	1 tablespoon	1 tablespoon	2 tablespoons	2 tablespoons

Grease a round or square cake tin thoroughly and line it with a double layer of greaseproof paper. Cream the butter and sugar together until light and fluffy. Beat in the black treacle. Add the eggs one at a time, adding a little of the flour with each egg after the first. Mix the flour with all the remaining ingredients except the brandy and orange juice, and gradually fold into the creamed mixture. Stir in the brandy and orange juice.

Place the mixture in the tin and smooth the top, using the back of a hot, wet metal spoon. Protect the cake from burning by tying a double layer of newspaper or brown paper round the outside and protruding above the rim and bake in a cool oven (140 C, 275 F, gas 1). Check the cake after the first 3 hours, then at intervals after that. The cake is done when it begins to shrink from the sides and a skewer inserted into it comes out clean. Leave it in the tin to cool completely before turning out.

To keep the cake moist and give a good flavour, prick the base of the cooked, upturned cake with a skewer and pour over a little brandy. Stand on a wire tray for a few hours to allow the brandy to penetrate. Wrap the cake well and store in an airtight tin. It will keep for up to six months.

Star Christmas Cake

6-egg quantity Victoria Sandwich cake mixture (page 77)
1 (150-g/5.29-oz) bar white chocolate
2 tablespoons hundreds and thousands
3 quantities fudge icing (page 81)
30-cm/12-in round cake board

Grease and base line two 25-cm/10-in Victoria sandwich tins. Prepare the cake mixture according to the recipe instructions, but with such a large quantity you might find it easier to make two batches. Spoon the mixture into the prepared tins and level the surface. Bake in a moderate oven (180C, 350F, gas4) for 40–45 minutes or until well risen and firm to the touch. Cool in the tins for a few minutes then turn on to wire racks to cool completely.

Meanwhile melt the chocolate in a basin over a saucepan of hot water. Spread a thin coat of chocolate on a piece of waxed or non-stick baking parchment. Sprinkle evenly with the hundreds and thousands and leave to set. Cut into pieces using a star-shaped cutter.

Following the diagrams, make a paper pattern and use to cut around the edges of the cake.

Place half of the cake on the cake board, spread with a quarter of the fudge icing then place the second half of cake on top. Cover the top and sides of the cake with the remaining icing, swirling it on with a palette knife. Before the icing sets decorate it with the sugar stars.

Chocolate Snowman

3-egg quantity Victoria Sandwich cake mixture (page 77)
50 g/2 oz apricot jam
2 quantities American Frosting (page 81)
a few Smarties
paper hat (optional)

Thoroughly grease one 300-ml/½-pint basin and one 900-ml/1½-pint basin. Prepare the cake mixture according to the recipe instructions, divide it between the two basins and bake in a moderate oven (160 C, 325 F, gas 3) for 1 hour 20 minutes for the small cake and 1 hour 25 minutes for the larger cake. Turn out and cool on a wire rack.

Trim the smaller cake around the wider edge to round it off slightly so that it will sit securely on the base. Spread the jam on top of the larger cake and place the small cake on top. Cover the cake completely in frosting. Place chocolate Smarties on the head to form eyes and halved red Smarties to form a mouth and nose. Place a few Smarties on the body to represent buttons. The snowman may have a paper hat on his head if desired.

Christmas Tree Cake

(Illustrated on page 123)

20-cm/8-in round cake tin quantity rich fruit cake (page 116)
350 g/12 oz almond paste (page 115)
food colourings
225 g/8 oz sieved apricot jam
¼ quantity royal icing (page 115)
100 g/4 oz flaked almonds, toasted
· 25-cm/10-in cake board

Grease and line a 20-cm/8-in round cake tin and make two or three paper piping bags according to the instructions on page 67. Prepare the cake mixture as detailed in the recipe instructions, spoon it into the prepared tin and smooth the surface, making a slight hollow in the centre. Wrap a double thickness of brown paper or newspaper around the tin, protruding above the rim, and secure with string. Bake the cake according to the instructions and leave it in the tin to cool completely before turning out.

Place the cake tin on a piece of paper and draw round it. Cut the shape out just inside the pencil outline to give you a round to fit the top of the cake. Draw in a Christmas tree following *Diagram 1* and cut carefully around each section.

Divide the almond paste into three. Leave one portion uncoloured, and colour the second dark green. Divide the third portion into three or four pieces and knead in different colours including brown and red. Roll out each colour on a board lightly dusted with icing sugar. Using the paper templates as a guide cut each piece from the appropriate colour. From the scraps cut a star for the top of the tree, a number of square parcels and round baubles using an upturned icing nozzle.

Place the cake on the cake board. Warm the apricot jam and brush a little evenly over the top of the cake. Carefully lift the pieces of almond paste on to a rolling pin and position over the top of the cake. When all the main pieces are in place gently roll over the surface with a rolling pin to smooth the joins. Then stick each parcel and bauble down with a dab of apricot jam.

Divide the royal icing into two or three portions, colour appropriately and use to fill the paper piping bags fitted with No.

2 writing nozzles. Pipe ribbons on the parcels and streamers on the tree. Warm the remaining apricot jam and spread around the side of the cake. Press on the flaked almonds using a palette knife.

Chocolate Yule Log

1 Chocolate Swiss Roll (page 103), unfilled
1½ quantities chocolate butter icing (page 80)
½ quantity almond paste (page 115)
red and green food colourings
icing sugar for sprinkling

Fill the Swiss roll with a third of the butter cream and place it on a plate. Put the remaining butter cream in a piping bag fitted with a large star nozzle or a large vegetable nozzle and pipe rings on either end of the Swiss roll. Now pipe lines along the roll to resemble bark on the log and small flat spirals for knotholes.

Colour a little almond paste bright red and roll it into tiny balls for holly berries. Colour the rest leafy green and make four small holly leaves. Cut the remaining paste into ivy leaves, either freehand, or using a picture from a Christmas card as a guide. Mark veins on the leaves with a knife.

Arrange all the leaves and berries on the log and sprinkle the whole lightly with icing sugar.

Christmas Tree Cookies

(Illustrated opposite)

450 g/1 lb plain flour
½ teaspoon salt
275 g/10 oz butter
225 g/8 oz icing sugar
2 eggs, lightly beaten
Decoration
3–4 egg yolks
food colourings (red, green, yellow etc)
pieces of gold string or narrow ribbon

Lightly grease three baking trays. Sift the flour and salt into a bowl. Rub in the butter until the mixture resembles fine bread-crumbs. Stir in the icing sugar, then add the beaten eggs and mix well to make a firm dough.

Knead lightly, then roll the dough out on a floured surface to a thickness of 5 mm/¼ in. Use Christmas cutters, for example, star, Christmas tree and animal shapes, to cut the dough. With a skewer, make a hole near the top of each cookie then carefully transfer them all to the prepared baking trays. Chill for at least 30 minutes.

Partially bake the cookies in a moderate oven (180 C, 350 F, gas 4) for 8 minutes. Place each egg yolk in a separate bowl and mix each one with a different food colouring to give a good strong colour. Using a soft artist's brush, paint the colours on to the cookies, then cook for a further 10 minutes.

Cool the cookies on a wire rack. When cold thread the ribbon through the holes and hang the cookies on the tree.
MAKES ABOUT 80

Christmas Tree Cake (page 120) with Almond-topped Mince Pies
(page 125) and Christmas Tree Cookies

Mince Pies

225 g/8 oz Shortcrust Pastry (page 9)
175 g/6 oz mincemeat
icing sugar to dredge

Lightly grease a tray of 12 patty tins. Prepare the pastry following the recipe instructions, knead lightly and roll out thinly on a floured board. Cut out 12 large rounds using a 6-cm/2½-in fluted cutter and 12 smaller rounds with a 5-cm/2-in fluted cutter, kneading and re-rolling the scraps of dough as necessary.

Press the larger rounds into the prepared patty tins and place a spoonful of mincemeat in each. Be careful not to overfill the mince pies. Dampen the edges of the smaller pastry rounds. Put them on top, pressing the edges tightly together, then prick each tart with a fork. Bake in a moderately hot oven (200 C, 400 F, gas 6) for 15–20 minutes or until lightly browned. Cool in the tins for a few minutes then transfer to a wire rack to cool completely, or serve warm. MAKES 12

Variations

Mallow Mince Pies: Use 100 g/4 oz shortcrust pastry to make the base of the mince pies only. Bake in the usual way but top each pie with a marshmallow 5 minutes before the end of the baking time.

Almond-topped Mince Pies *(Illustrated on page 123)*: Use 100 g/4 oz shortcrust pastry to make the base of the mince pies only. Roll out 100 g/4 oz almond paste and cut out 12 stars, place on top of the filled mince pies and bake in the usual way.

Easter Bunny Cake with Easter Nests (pages 127 and 128) and Bonnet Biscuits for Easter (page 128)

Hot Cross Buns

450 g/1 lb plain flour
50 g/2 oz caster sugar plus 1 teaspoon
1 tablespoon dried yeast
150 ml/¼ pint lukewarm milk
5 tablespoons warm water
1 teaspoon salt
½ teaspoon each mixed spice, cinnamon and nutmeg
100 g/4 oz currants
25–50 g/1–2 oz chopped mixed peel
50 g/2 oz butter, melted
1 egg, beaten
To glaze
2 tablespoons milk
2 tablespoons water
40 g/1½ oz caster sugar

Sift 100 g/4 oz of the flour with one teaspoon sugar, crumble in the yeast and stir in the mixed milk and water. Leave in a warm place until frothy, about 20–30 minutes. Sift together the remaining flour, salt, spices and sugar; add the fruit. Stir the butter and egg into the yeast batter, add the flour and fruit and mix well. Knead the dough on a floured surface for about 10 minutes.

Divide the dough into 12 pieces and shape into buns by using the palm of one hand, first pressing down hard and then easing up. Place on a floured baking tray spaced well apart, put the baking tray inside a greased polythene bag and leave the buns to rise at room temperature for about 45 minutes before removing the bag. Make a cross with a very sharp knife to just cut the surface of the dough. Bake in a hot oven (220 C, 425 F, gas 7) for 15–20 minutes. Cool on a wire rack.

For the glazing, bring the milk and the water to the boil, stir in the sugar and boil for 2 minutes. Brush buns twice while still warm. MAKES 12

Easter Bunny Cake

(Illustrated on page 124)

4-egg quantity Victoria Sandwich cake mixture (page 77)
double quantity Butter Icing (page 80)
pink food colouring · 1 chocolate button
6 long Matchmakers · 2 liquorice sweets
3 Smarties · bow of pink ribbon
50 g/2 oz desiccated coconut, coloured green
a few flower cake decorations
30-cm/12-in square cake board

Grease and line a 33 × 18-cm/13 × 7-in Swiss roll tin. Prepare the cake mixture according to the recipe instructions, spoon it into the prepared tin and level the surface. Bake in a moderate oven (180 C, 350 F, gas 5) for 30–35 minutes or until well risen and firm to the touch. Cool in the tin for a few minutes before turning out on to a wire rack to cool completely.

Following the diagram on page 132, cut out a paper rabbit and use this as a guide for cutting the cake. Put the cake on the board. Colour about one-third of the icing pink. Cover the body of the bunny completely in white butter icing, then cover the middle of the ears, tail and paws with pink icing. Add two liquorice sweets for eyes, a chocolate button for a nose, the Matchmakers for whiskers and three Smarties for buttons. Put a bow on the bunny to finish the decoration.

Sprinkle the green coconut on the board around the bunny and add the flower cake decorations.

Easter Nests

(Illustrated on page 124)

1-egg quantity chocolate Victoria Sandwich mixture (page 77)
½ quantity chocolate butter icing (page 80)
24 small sugar or chocolate eggs

Place eight paper cake cases in a patty tin tray. Prepare the cake mixture following the recipe instructions and divide between the paper cases. Bake in a moderately hot oven (190 C, 375 F, gas 5) for 15–20 minutes or until well risen and firm to the touch. Remove the buns from the tray and turn out on to a wire rack to cool.

Spoon the icing into a nylon piping bag fitted with a small star nozzle. Pipe a ring of chocolate icing around the edge of each cake to form a nest. Place three eggs in each nest before serving.
MAKES 8

Bonnet Biscuits for Easter

(Illustrated on page 124)

Biscuit dough
75 g/3 oz margarine · 100 g/4 oz plain flour
100 g/4 oz ground almonds
75 g/3 oz caster sugar · 1 egg, lightly beaten
Decoration
1 quantity vanilla butter icing (page 80)
100 g/4 oz marshmallows
pink and yellow food colourings
sugar flowers, fruit dragees
small bows of baby ribbon

Lightly grease two baking trays and make two greaseproof paper piping bags following the instructions on page 67. Rub the margarine into the flour until the mixture resembles fine breadcrumbs. Stir in the remaining dough ingredients and knead together lightly.

Roll the dough out to a thickness of 3 mm/⅛ in. Cut it into

rounds using a 6-cm/2½-in round cutter and carefully transfer the rounds to the prepared baking trays.

Bake in a moderate oven (180 C, 350 F, gas 4) for about 15–20 minutes or until lightly browned. Allow the biscuits to cool slightly on the trays, then transfer to a wire rack until cold.

While the biscuits are cooling, make the butter icing according to the recipe instructions. Secure a marshmallow on top of each biscuit with a little butter icing. Colour half the remaining butter icing pink and the second half yellow. Spoon one colour into each of the paper piping bags, fitted with small star nozzles. Pipe a ring of pink or yellow rosettes round each marshmallow. Add edible decorations and small bows made with the ribbon to imitate a fancy hat as shown in the picture. MAKES 18

Pumpkin Pie

(Illustrated on page 133)

225 g/8 oz Sweet Flan Pastry (page 10)
Filling
350 g/12 oz pumpkin flesh, chopped
100 g/4 oz demerara sugar · 2 teaspoons cinnamon
2 teaspoons nutmeg · 2 teaspoons ginger · 2 eggs, beaten
150 ml/¼ pint milk
grated rind and juice of 1 lemon
Decoration
150 ml/¼ pint double cream, whipped

Make the pastry following the recipe instructions and use to line a 20-cm/8-in flan tin or dish.

Steam the chopped pumpkin for about 25 minutes until tender then mash well or purée in a blender or food processor.

Beat in the sugar and spices. Gradually add the eggs, milk, lemon juice and rind, beating all the time. Pour the mixture into the pastry case.

Bake in a moderately hot oven (190 C, 375 F, gas 5) for 1 hour. Allow to cool and serve decorated with rosettes of whipped cream. SERVES 6

Trick or Treat Biscuits

*The 'trick' to these biscuits is the hidden layer of
orange marzipan.*

100 g/4 oz butter or margarine
100 g/4 oz soft light brown sugar
3 tablespoons golden syrup · 1 egg, lightly beaten
50 g/2 oz chocolate vermicelli
350 g/12 oz plain flour, sieved
Topping and decoration
grated rind of 1 orange
½ quantity almond paste (page 115)
a little icing sugar
100 g/4 oz apricot jam
350 g/12 oz plain chocolate

Lightly grease two baking trays. Cream the butter or margarine
with the sugar and syrup until very soft, light and fluffy. Gradually add the egg, beating continuously, then work in the chocolate vermicelli and flour with the back of a wooden spoon. Knead
the mixture gently, then roll it out on a floured board to a
thickness of 5 mm/¼ in. Cut the dough into rounds with a 7.5-cm/
3-in plain cutter. Carefully transfer the rounds to the prepared
baking trays, spacing them a little apart to allow room for
spreading. Chill for 30 minutes or longer if you have time.

Bake in a moderate oven (180 C, 350 F, gas 4) for 20 minutes or
until lightly brown. Remove the hot biscuits from the trays and
turn out on to a wire rack to cool completely.

Meanwhile, knead the orange rind into the marzipan then roll
out thinly on a surface lightly sprinkled with icing sugar, and cut
into 7.5-cm/3-in rounds. Warm the apricot jam and brush evenly
over the top of each biscuit, then sandwich the biscuits together
with the marzipan rounds. Melt the chocolate in a basin over a
saucepan of hot water then, using two forks, dip in each biscuit.
Leave to set on a piece of waxed paper or non-stick baking
parchment before serving. MAKES 24

Bonfire-night Flapjacks

(Illustrated on page 133)

100 g/4 oz margarine
4 tablespoons golden syrup
75 g/3 oz granulated sugar
225 g/8 oz rolled oats
$\frac{1}{4}$ teaspoon salt

Grease a square, shallow tin, about 20 cm/8 in. Put the margarine and syrup in a pan and leave over a low heat until the margarine has melted. Remove from the heat and add the sugar, rolled oats and salt. Mix thoroughly. Turn the mixture into the prepared tin and cook in a moderate oven (160 C, 325 F, gas 3) for 30–40 minutes until golden brown.

Leave to cool in tin for 5 minutes then cut 12 bars while still in the tin. (If they are allowed to get cold they cannot be cut, and will just break into pieces.) Turn out on to a wire rack to cool completely. MAKES 12

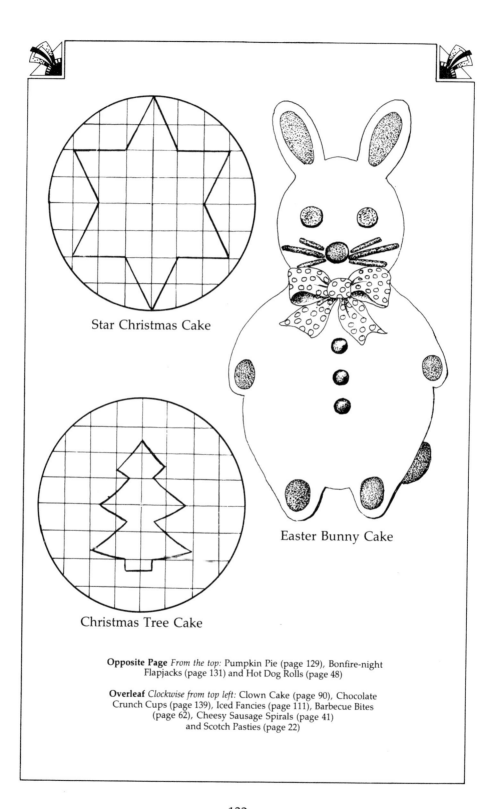

Star Christmas Cake

Christmas Tree Cake

Easter Bunny Cake

Opposite Page *From the top:* Pumpkin Pie (page 129), Bonfire-night Flapjacks (page 131) and Hot Dog Rolls (page 48)

Overleaf *Clockwise from top left:* Clown Cake (page 90), Chocolate Crunch Cups (page 139), Iced Fancies (page 111), Barbecue Bites (page 62), Cheesy Sausage Spirals (page 41) and Scotch Pasties (page 22)

Sweets and Cookies Children Can Make

Little girls and boys alike all love to help mummy in the kitchen, making pastry and getting into a sticky mess with cake mixture. This is when they begin to learn the art of survival in the kitchen and they will probably enjoy it most before they have to rely on their own talents!

So encourage your children to join you when you are cooking; they will enjoy helping and they can also learn to make delightful edible gifts. Encourage older children to work on their own but do stay in the kitchen to make sure that all is safe and well. With a little patience, a large apron and a selection of ingredients great fun can be had by all!

Opposite Page *Clockwise from top left:* Uncooked Coconut Ice (page 140), Jam Tarts (page 139), Cherry and Walnut Biscuits (page 140), Peppermint Creams (page 141) and Cake Truffles (page 142)

137

Chocolate Nut Rocks

225 g/8 oz plain flour · ½ teaspoon salt
2 teaspoons baking powder · 65 g/2½ oz butter
65 g/2½ oz sugar · 50 g/2 oz chocolate chips
50 g/2 oz walnut pieces · ¼ teaspoon nutmeg
1 egg · 2 tablespoons milk

Grease a baking tray. Sieve the flour, salt and baking powder together. Rub the fat into the flour until the mixture resembles fine breadcrumbs. Stir in the sugar, chocolate chips, walnuts and nutmeg. Beat the egg with the milk and add to the flour mixture. Mix well with a fork; the mixture should be stiff but not too sticky and should leave the sides of the mixing bowl clean.

Put the mixture in 12 separate heaps on the greased tray, roughing them up with a fork. Bake in a moderately hot oven (200 C, 400 F, gas 6) for 15–20 minutes. Turn out on to a wire rack to cool. MAKES 12

A tip: Rock cakes are not rich and so are best eaten on the same day. For a crunchy topping, sprinkle with demerara sugar before baking.

Simple Mother's Day Cake

Children love to prepare a cake for their mothers and the recipe for Refrigerator Cake (page 112) is ideal for them to make as it does not involve cooking.

When the mixture is prepared, press it into the tin and leave it to set in the refrigerator. Make 1 quantity Glacé Icing (page 80). Spread the icing on top of the cake but not around the sides. Tie a large bow of ribbon around the cake. To decorate the cake put a small bunch of flowers in the middle – these can be material flowers bought from a florist (or lots of shops sell them), a few crystallised violets and some sugar mimosa balls or other cake decorations.

Jam Tarts

(Illustrated on page 136)

100 g/4 oz Shortcrust Pastry (page 9)
175 g/6 oz strawberry jam

Lightly grease a tray of 12 patty tins. Prepare the pastry according to the recipe instructions, but using half the quantities. Knead lightly and roll out thinly on a floured board. Cut into rounds using a 6-cm/2½-in fluted cutter. Press each round gently into the prepared patty tins then place a small spoonful of jam in each, be careful not to overfill them. Bake in a moderately hot oven (200 C, 400 F, gas 6) for about 15–20 minutes or until the pastry is lightly browned. Cool in the tins for a few minutes and then turn out on to a wire rack to cool completely. MAKES ABOUT 12

Chocolate Crunch Cups

(Illustrated on pages 134/135)

100 g/4 oz plain or milk chocolate
40 g/1½ oz butter or margarine
2 tablespoons golden syrup
40 g/1½ oz cornflakes

Arrange eight paper cake cases on a baking tray. Break the chocolate into pieces and place in a bowl over a saucepan of hot water together with the margarine and syrup. Heat gently, stirring occasionally until melted, then stir in the cornflakes. Using a spoon and fork divide the mixture between the paper cases and leave in a cool place until set. MAKES 8

Cherry and Walnut Biscuits

(Illustrated on page 136)

175 g/6 oz margarine · 150 g/5 oz soft brown sugar
1 egg, beaten · 1 teaspoon vanilla essence
275 g/10 oz self-raising flour
50 g/2 oz walnuts, chopped
75 g/3 oz glacé cherries

Grease two baking trays. Cream the margarine and sugar together until light and fluffy and beat in the egg, vanilla essence and flour. Add the walnuts and half the cherries, chopped finely, and mix well. Form the mixture into small balls and place them on the prepared baking trays – a little apart to allow room for spreading. Press the balls flat with a knife and put a piece of cherry into the centre of each one. Bake in a moderate oven (180 C, 350 F, gas 4) for 20 minutes. Lift off the trays carefully and turn on to a wire rack to cool. MAKES ABOUT 50

Uncooked Coconut Ice

(Illustrated on page 136)

10 tablespoons full-cream sweetened condensed milk
225 g/8 oz icing sugar, sifted
175 g/6 oz desiccated coconut · pink food colouring

Mix together the condensed milk, all the icing sugar except 1 tablespoon and the coconut. The mixture will be thick so should be mixed very vigorously. Remove half the mixture from the bowl and shape into a neat oblong 20 × 15 cm/8 × 6 in. Add the colouring to the remaining mixture, blend well then shape into another oblong the same as the first. Put this on to the white oblong and press the two together firmly. Dust a flat tin with the remaining icing sugar. Place the coconut ice on this, leave until firm then cut into neat squares. MAKES 24

Mallow Dippers

175 g/6 oz milk chocolate · 2 tablespoons golden syrup
50 g/2 oz butter or margarine · grated rind of 1 orange
1 (227-g/8-oz) packet marshmallows

Break the chocolate into pieces and place in a bowl over a saucepan of hot water together with the syrup, butter or margarine and orange rind. Heat gently, stirring occasionally, until melted. Allow to cool slightly. To serve, spear a marshmallow with a wooden skewer and dip into the warm chocolate.

Simple Chocolates

Children love to make simple edible gifts; easiest of all are fruits and marzipan shapes dipped in chocolate. Strawberries, small acorns of marzipan, mandarin segments, whole shelled nuts and small rounds of fondant icing can all be dipped in melted chocolate. For economy, use melted chocolate cake covering which is less likely to separate if it is overheated. Make sure the child is well covered with a large apron and stay near to supervise the operation!

Peppermint Creams

(Illustrated on page 136)

225 g/8 oz icing sugar, plus a little for sprinkling
1 egg white · peppermint essence

Sift the icing sugar into a bowl and mix with enough egg white to form a stiff paste. Add a few drops of peppermint essence and knead the paste lightly with the tips of your fingers. Roll it out to a thickness of about 5 mm/¼ in on a surface sprinkled with icing sugar, and stamp out 2.5-cm/1-in rounds or shapes with a cutter. Leave to dry for 24 hours. MAKES ABOUT 25

Cake Truffles

(Illustrated on page 136)

50 g/2 oz butter · 50 g/2 oz caster sugar
few drops of almond essence · 75 g/3 oz ground almonds
2 teaspoons cocoa powder · 50 g/2 oz cake crumbs, sieved
orange juice · chocolate vermicelli for coating

Cream the butter and sugar until soft and fluffy. Add the almond essence, ground almonds and cocoa. Beat thoroughly. Mix in sufficient cake crumbs to form a stiff paste. Add a few drops of orange juice to flavour the mixture.

Knead well and roll into a sausage shape, then cut into equal-sized pieces, roll each into a ball, and roll each ball in chocolate vermicelli. MAKES 12

Chocolate Nut Logs

If the children are using the cooker, then stay in the room to supervise them and avoid any accidents.

175 g/6 oz milk or plain chocolate
100 g/4 oz crunchy peanut butter
50 g/2 oz butter or margarine
225 g/8 oz icing sugar, sieved

Break the chocolate into pieces and place in a bowl over a saucepan of hot water together with the peanut butter and butter or margarine. Heat gently, stirring occasionally, until melted. Remove from the heat and allow to cool for 10 minutes then beat in the icing sugar. Leave until the mixture is firm enough to handle then shape into 7.5-cm/3-in long shapes with wetted hands. Chill in the fridge for 1 hour before serving. MAKES 20

Index